# WE, THE

MW01051764

## A HELP TO UNDERSTANDING THE CHURCH ORDER

**CRC PUBLICATIONS**
Grand Rapids, Michigan

**Acknowledgments**

This book is prepared by the Education, Worship, and Evangelism Department of CRC Publications in consultation with the office of the general secretary of the Christian Reformed Church in North America. This work includes the Church Order revisions adopted/ratified by Synod 1995 of the Christian Reformed Church.

The editors wish to thank Henry De Moor, Jr., professor of church polity at Calvin Theological Seminary; David Engelhard, general secretary of the Christian Reformed Church; and Leonard J. Hofman, former general secretary, for their help in reviewing and shaping this document.

We, the Church
A Help to Understanding the Church Order

ISBN: 1-56212-118-9

Printed in the United States of America on recycled paper. ⊕

# Contents

# Foreword

Through the years, we, the Christian Reformed Church in North America, have followed a set of rules that has helped us to organize ourselves and carry out our activities in an orderly way, in line with the teachings of the Word of God. These rules are known as the Church Order of the Christian Reformed Church (CRC).

Those of us who have been members of the CRC since childhood are more or less familiar with the terms and language of the Church Order. But those of us who are new Christians, who have come from various cultural backgrounds, or who have come into the CRC from other churches are not as familiar with those rules.

Therefore, we have prepared this "help to understanding the Church Order" to make it easier for all of us to understand how we govern ourselves. It is written in a conversational style, in the way that people would talk about the Church Order in everyday language.

This help should be used alongside the Church Order (included at the back of this book) so that we can become better acquainted with the official language of the rules that have been approved by the synod of the Christian Reformed Church.

May God bless the use of this tool so that it may help us to a better understanding of who we are and what our ministry together is.

—Leonard J. Hofman

# Glossary

admonition—shepherd-like advice and warning to members who have sinned in their teaching or in their Christian walk. (See Art. 78-84; 1 Pet. 5:1-4.)

assembly, assemblies—gathering of church leaders. The assemblies of the CRC are the **council**, the **classis**, and the **synod**. (See Art. 26-50.)

baptism—one of the **sacraments** of the church. Children or adults may be baptized with water in the name of God the Father, God the Son, and God the Holy Spirit. Children of believing parents should be baptized as infants. The CRC views baptism as a sign and seal of God's promise for our salvation. (See also Acts 2:38-39; Romans 6:4; Colossians 2:12.)

baptized members—children or adults who have received the **sacrament** of **baptism** in the CRC.

board of trustees—a group of people chosen to supervise. In this booklet, the term *Board of Trustees* refers to the board that watches over **Calvin Theological Seminary**. (See Art. 19.)

Calvin College—the official college of the CRC.

Calvin Theological Seminary—the official school for training **ministers** in the CRC. (See Art. 19.)

candidate—a person who is qualified to be a **minister** in the CRC. A candidate must be **ordained** before he can begin work as a minister of the Word.

catechism—see **Heidelberg Catechism**.

chaplain—a minister who is called to ministry in the military or in an institution or other organization. (See Art. 12-c.)

church visitors—the church visitors are appointed by the **classis** to visit all the churches in the classis each year. They visit to see how things are going in the local church. They may also meet with a **council** when it wants advice or needs help with problems. (See Art. 42.)

classis, classes—the classis is the **assembly** that is made up of several churches in one area. Delegates from all the classes go to **synod**. (See Art. 27-34, 39-44.)

*colloquium doctum*—this Latin term means "doctrinal conversation." This is an exam that a **candidate** must pass before he can be **ordained** as a minister in the CRC. (See Supplement, Art. 8, 10.)

confessing adult members—those who are at least 18 years old and who have made a commitment to the Reformed creeds and to the responsibilities of adult membership. These responsibilities may include the right to vote and the right to hold **office** and to serve in other ways as leaders in the church. (See Art. 59.)

confessing members—those who have been baptized and have professed their faith in Jesus Christ. Confessing members may take part in celebrating the **Lord's Supper**. (See Art. 59.)

confessions—see **Heidelberg Catechism.**

confidentiality—in general, this means respect for someone's privacy in terms of personal information they have shared with you. Guidelines for confidentiality in the church are given in the Church Order **Supplement** (for Art. 78-84). Those guidelines apply to any matters that deal with advice, counseling, or discipline. Church members must be able to trust their **council** with private matters. In other words, a person on the council may not go around talking about someone's confidential information.

congregation—the body of believers in a local church.

consistory—this part of the **council** is made up of the elders and minister (or ministers). (See Art. 35-b.)

council—this **assembly** is made up of the elders, deacons, and minister (or ministers). (See Art. 35-38.)

counselor—a person who is assigned to help a local church as it looks for a new **minister.** (See Art. 9.)

CRC agency—an organization that carries out ministry in the name of the CRC. The CRC agencies are given their tasks by **synod**.

creed—a statement of faith accepted by the church. The CRC uses the Apostles' Creed, the Nicene Creed, and the Athanasian Creed. There are also three forms of unity, also known as the Reformed confessions: the Belgic Confession, the **Heidelberg Catechism**, and the Canons of Dort.

deacon—a person who serves in a local church to help people in need. (See Art. 25, 35-c.)

delegate—an elder or minister who is sent to a meeting of classis or synod. A delegate has the authority to speak for his church or classis. He may also vote at the meeting. (See Art. 27, 34.)

denomination—a group of churches that unite to work together under Christ, such as the CRC.

depose, deposition—to remove a person from **office** permanently, for the purpose of **discipline**. (See Art. 82-84.)

diaconal committee—a committee that works to help people in need. A committee like this does work that goes beyond the limits of the local-church deacons. A classis may have a diaconal committee. Synod also has a diaconal committee—it is called the Christian Reformed World Relief Committee (CRWRC).

diaconate—the body of the **deacons** in a local church.

director of finances—the person who keeps track of the finances of synod and the CRC agencies.

discipline—the shepherd-like act of correcting church members who have sinned in their teaching or their Christian walk. (See Art. 78-84; 1 Pet. 5:1-4.)

doctrine—church teachings about the Bible, God, the church, sin, and salvation.

dogmatics—the study of teachings about **doctrine.**

ecumenical synod—large meeting of many different churches.

elder—a person who serves in the local church to give pastoral care and to make decisions for the church. (See Art. 25, 35-b.)

evangelist—an **elder** who is called to help a group of believers become a church. (See Art. 23-24.)

evangelize, evangelism—when you evangelize, you share the good news of Jesus Christ with someone else. The purpose of evangelism is to spread God's word of salvation everywhere. Then people may believe in Jesus and be saved.

excommunicate—to separate a person from official fellowship in the church. This may be done only when a person has separated himself or herself from God by sinful actions and does not want to repent. (See Art. 67-68, 78-84.)

exegesis—explanation of the text of the Old and New Testaments.

exhort—to explain the Word of God.

fellowship—being together in Christ as part of the worldwide body of believers; *in fellowship* means sharing the same beliefs and similar teachings. (See also Acts 2:42-47.)

Form of Subscription—a statement that binds all officebearers (ministers of the Word, evangelists, elders, deacons) and **professors** in the CRC. When you sign this form, you show that you believe God's Word and the teachings of the Reformed confessions. You also promise to submit to authority if someday you disagree with a teaching of the church.

Fund for Smaller Churches—a committee that helps churches that do not have enough funds to support themselves.

general secretary—the official representative of the CRC to the government and to the churches.

good standing—Members in good standing are those who are living as they should and who have not been placed under discipline by the church consistory.

Heidelberg Catechism—one of the confessions of the Reformed faith. The questions and answers of this confession are divided into 52 "Lord's Days," one for each Sunday of the year. The other two confessions used by the CRC are the Belgic Confession and the Canons of Dort.

install—to place a person in a specific position for the work of the church, often for a certain time period.

interim committee—a group of persons that may make decisions for a **classis** or **synod** while it is not in session. The classis or synod appoints the members of this committee. (See Art. 33.)

just objection—a just objection offers a reason (related to beliefs or lifestyle) why a person may not be able to serve the church well. But it would not be "just" to object if you simply did not like a person.

lapse of membership—a person whose membership is lapsed is no longer a member of a local church. (See Supplement, Art. 67.)

Lord's Supper—one of the **sacraments** of the CRC. **Confessing members** may celebrate the Lord's Supper. They eat bread and drink wine (or juice) as a reminder that Christ gave his body and blood for our salvation. (See also Luke 22:14-20; 1 Corinthians 11:23-26.)

minister—a minister of the Word and sacraments, **ordained** to preach the Word of God and to lead in the celebration of the **sacraments.** (See Art. 6-22.)

ministry share—a set amount that churches give to support the classis and the denomination.

missionary—a person who is called to do work in missions.

mutual censure—at least four times a year the **council** members review their work together. They do this to build each other up, to discuss any problems they may have with each other, and to pray for the Lord's healing and help in their work together for the local church.

office—a public position of duty and leadership in the church. A person in office is part of the **council** of the local church. A person in office must be **ordained** as a **minister** of the Word, an **evangelist,** an **elder,** or a **deacon.**

ordain, ordination—to appoint a person to a specific task in the church, such as the **office** of minister, evangelist, elder, or deacon.

organized church—a church that is able to govern itself, support itself, and reach out into its community. An organized church needs to be led by a minister of the Word in the CRC.

pastor—a **minister** of the Word who does pastoral care in the local church.

Presbyterian, presbytery—a Presbyterian church is one that is governed by elders. A presbytery is a gathering of ministers and elders—similar to the CRC **classis**. There are several Presbyterian **denominations**. They are closely related to the Reformed churches.

profession of faith—the act of declaring your faith in public. In the CRC you do this in a **public worship** service. You state your faith in Christ and promise to follow him always.

professor—in this book, the word *professor* refers to those who are professors at Calvin College or Calvin Theological Seminary, the official college and seminary of the CRC. (See Art. 20.)

public worship—a regular worship service in the CRC. It is open to anyone who wants to come. Public worship is held at least twice on Sunday. It is also held on the Christian holidays, days of prayer, and days of thanksgiving.

sacraments—the CRC has two sacraments—**baptism** and the **Lord's Supper** (Holy Communion). A minister of the Word may baptize children and adults. He may also lead the church in celebrating the Lord's Supper.

Supplement—a document that helps explain parts of the Church Order. This *Help to Understanding the Church Order* includes the information from the Supplement that goes with articles of the Church Order.

suspend, suspension—to remove from **office** for a period of time, for the purpose of **discipline**. (See Art. 82-84.)

synod—a meeting of **elders** and **ministers** from all the **classes** in the CRC. Synod meets once a year to make decisions for all the local churches. Synod is the largest **assembly** of the CRC. (See Art. 26-34, 45-50.)

synodical deputies—**ministers** who are appointed by **synod** to help the **classes** make decisions. (See Art. 48.)

# A HELP TO UNDERSTANDING THE CHURCH ORDER

## Introduction

### The Purpose and Basis of the Church Order

We are the Christian Reformed Church (CRC). We submit totally to God's Word, the Bible. We believe that the Reformed **creeds** are a true explanation of God's Word. We accept Jesus Christ as the only Head of the church. We also want to do everything decently and in order, as the Bible tells us to (1 Corinthians 14:40). Because we believe all this, we have set up the Church Order as our constitution.

The contents of the Church Order are

- Part 1: The **Offices** of the Church
- Part 2: The **Assemblies** of the Church
- Part 3: The Work and Activities of the Church
- Part 4: The **Admonition** and **Discipline** of the Church.

—see Church Order, Art. 1

### Part 1: The Offices of the Church

### A. General Information

### The Special Offices in the Church

The CRC calls its members to serve in four types of **office**:

- **minister** of the Word **(pastor)**
- **evangelist**
- **elder**
- **deacon**

These offices must be equally respected.

—see Church Order, Art. 2

---

Words in **boldface** type are explained in a glossary at the beginning of this book. The Church Order itself (1994 edition) is printed at the back of this book (gray pages). Supplements to the Church Order are printed in the book *Church Order/ Rules for Synodical Procedure.*

### Members Who May Serve in the Special Offices

Men who are **confessing adult members** of the church may serve as ministers, evangelists, or elders. They must also meet the Bible's requirements for these offices. (Some of these requirements are found in 1 Timothy 3:1-7 and Titus 1:6-9.)

Synod 1995 declared that a **classis** may decide also to have women serve as ministers, evangelists, or elders. **Synod** made several rules in connection with this situation:

- The **general secretary** will keep a list of all the classes that make this decision.
- A classis may not send women **delegates** to synod.
- A woman minister may not serve as a **synodical deputy**.
- A classis may decide *not* to have women serve as ministers, evangelists, or elders. But a local church in that classis may decide to have women elders who serve only within that local church.
- When a qualified woman applies to become a **candidate**, the persons who are to decide about the application will not be forced to take part, if that would go against their conscience.
- Synodical deputies will not be forced to take part in any matter related to ministers of the Word, if that would go against their conscience.
- A synodical **agency** may not appoint women as ministers of the Word. It also may not seek to have them **installed** by a local church.

All confessing adult members, men and women, may serve as deacons if they live up to the Bible's requirements for deacons. (Some of these requirements are found in 1 Timothy 3:8-13.)

To serve as a minister, elder, deacon, or evangelist, you must be called to that office by a local church. Then you must be **ordained** and **installed** to that office. (If you are called to that office for another term, you need to be installed again but not ordained again.)

—see Church Order, Art. 3; **Supplement**, Art. 3-a

### Calling to Special Offices

What is the process for calling and electing a person to serve in one of these offices?

First of all, the **council** comes up with a list of members who can serve in these offices. Then the council gives the list to the **congregation**. The list should usually have the names of at least twice as many people as are needed for each office. So if you need to elect three elders, the council will normally give the congregation at least six names to choose from. If the council does not give twice the number of names needed, it should explain why. *Exception:* For the churches in Classis Red Mesa, the council must come up with a list of one or more persons needed for each office.

Before it comes up with a list of names, the council may tell the congregation about positions that need to be filled. Then the congregation may name people who might be able to fill those positions.

After a word of prayer, the council oversees the election. The election goes by rules set up by the council. Only confessing adult members of the church in **good standing** may vote in the election.

The council tells everyone the names of the members who have been elected. If no one has any **just objection,** the council will **ordain** or **install** the persons to office. The council will do this when the congregation is gathered for **public worship**. The council will use the official forms for ordaining and installing persons to office.

—see Church Order, Art. 4; Supplement, Art. 4-a

### Signing the Form of Subscription

All those who hold office in the church are called *officebearers*. They must sign the **Form of Subscription**. People sign this form to show that they agree with the **doctrine,** or teachings, of the church. People must sign this form when they are first ordained or installed in a local church. They must also sign it when they go to a meeting of **classis** for the first time. They must also sign it when they go to **synod**.

The Form of Subscription is signed by **ministers, evangelists, elders, deacons,** and **professors** when they are ordained or installed in office, or both. A copy of this form is printed below:

*Form of Subscription*

We, the undersigned,
servants of the divine Word
    in the _____ Christian Reformed Church,
    in Classis _____,
by means of our signatures
declare truthfully and in good conscience before the Lord
    that we sincerely believe
    that all the articles and points of doctrine
        set forth in the Belgic Confession,
        the Heidelberg Catechism, and the Canons of Dort
    fully agree with the Word of God.
We promise therefore
    to teach these doctrines diligently,
    to defend them faithfully,
    and not to contradict them,
        publicly or privately,
        directly or indirectly,
        in our preaching, teaching, or writing.
We pledge moreover
    not only to reject all errors
        that conflict with these doctrines,
    but also to refute them,
    and to do everything we can
        to keep the church free from them.
We promise further that if in the future
    we come to have any difficulty with these doctrines
        or reach views differing from them,
    we will not propose, defend, preach, or teach such views,
        either publicly or privately,
        until we have first disclosed them

to the council, classis, or synod for examination.
We are prepared moreover
  to submit to the judgment
  of the council, classis, or synod,
    realizing that the consequence of refusal to do so
    is suspension from office.
We promise in addition
  that if, to maintain unity and purity in doctrine,
  the council, classis, or synod
  considers it proper at any time—
    on sufficient grounds of concern—
  to require a fuller explanation of our views
    concerning any article
    in the three confessions mentioned above,
  we are always willing and ready
    to comply with such a request,
    realizing here also that the consequence of refusal to do so
    is suspension from office.
Should we consider ourselves wronged, however,
  by the judgment of the council or classis,
we reserve for ourselves the right of appeal;
but until a decision is made on such an appeal,
  we will acquiesce in the determination and judgment
  already made.

—see Church Order, Art. 5; Supplement, Art. 5

### B. Ministers of the Word

#### Admission to the Ministry of the Word

To become a **minister** of the Word in the CRC, a person needs to be trained in theology and ministry. This training must meet all the requirements set by synod.

A person who wants to become a minister of the Word must graduate from **Calvin Theological Seminary**. He must also be declared a **candidate** for the ministry of the Word. Then he will be ready to receive a call to a local church.

Those who have studied at another seminary must meet certain requirements set by **synod**. Then they may be approved as candidates for the ministry of the Word. Then they will be ready to receive a call to a local church.

A person who wants to be a minister may study theology at another seminary. If he wants to be approved for ministry in the CRC, that person must at least take the senior year at Calvin Theological Seminary.

If a person has not been a full-time, regular student at the seminary, the seminary **Board of Trustees** needs to interview him. Before the interview, the board needs recommendations about him from the seminary professors. If he has studied at another seminary, the board also needs recommendations from his professors there. The recommendations must deal with his scholarship, faithfulness to the Reformed teachings, spiritual walk, and personality. If the board recommends him to synod, then synod will declare him a candidate.

Graduates of Calvin Seminary are normally declared as candidates at synod. Synod meets once a year. These rules must be followed if a student wants to become a candidate between the yearly synods:

1. If a student will not graduate before synod meets, he may still apply to become a candidate. He may do this when

    a. he has completed all core requirements for academic courses and field education, and

    b. he is within twelve hours of completing his course work, and

    c. he is within ten units of completing his field education.

2. When synod meets, it may declare that he can become a candidate when he completes all these requirements.

3. When he completes all these requirements, the executive committee of the Board of Trustees will inform the CRC **general secretary**. The general secretary will then announce that the candidate is approved and ready for a call.

4. Any student who does not complete all requirements by March 1 (before the next synod) must apply again to become a candidate. This student must re-apply to the secretary of the Board of Trustees.

5. Sometimes a candidate does not receive or accept a call by May 15 (before the next synod). If he still wants to be a candidate, he must reapply to the secretary of the Board of Trustees by May 15.

—see Church Order, Art. 6; Supplement, Art. 6;
see also Supplement, Art. 10

**Admission to the Ministry without the Usual Training**

If a person does not have training in theology, he may still be approved as a minister of the Word. His life must show that he has exceptional gifts of godliness, humbleness, spirituality, wisdom, and a natural ability to preach the Word. The approval of a person like this is *an exception to the rule*. This exception is usually made only when there is an urgent need for a minister.

This person must be examined by the **classis**. The **synodical deputies** must be present for this examination. The classis needs to make sure that this person has the exceptional gifts of ministry. The classis also has to make sure that this person needs to be approved at this time. If the classis and the synodical deputies agree to approve him, then classis may declare that he is ready for a call to the ministry. All this must be done in line with rules set up by synod.

*Becoming Approved without the Usual Training*

1. If a person wants to enter the ministry without the usual training, he must first apply to his **council** and then to classis. The classis, along with **delegates** from nearby classes, will examine this person. They will first look at statements that the council has written about him. These statements deal with his qualifications and the reason for approving him, as required by this process. The classis will decide whether there are enough reasons to accept his application for ministry.

If classis accepts the application, the person will be allowed to **exhort** (explain the Word of God) in churches that do not have **pastors**. He may do this for a set period of time. He will also be allowed to exhort a few times in churches that do have pastors, as long as those pastors are present. The "set period of time" is a probation period. During this time the classis will see how well the person does. Classis will decide how long this period will last.

2. At the end of the "set period of time," everyone who examined this person will make their final decision about his "exceptional gifts." If they decide that he does have the gifts, then they will examine him in these areas:

- explanation **(exegesis)** of the Old and New Testaments
- Bible history
- doctrine (**dogmatics,** church teachings)
- general and American church history

3. If the person does well in this exam, the classis may declare that he is ready for a call.

4. Another examination by classis will take place later, in line with the rules of synod. The candidate will not be tested in the ancient languages (Hebrew or Greek).

*Statements about Using This Process*

1. Synod reminds the churches that this process was established when there were not enough **ministers** to go around. This process should be used only in a time of great need.

2. The "exceptional gifts" of the person being examined must be truly exceptional. No one should be examined by way of this process if he is not unusually gifted.

3. The person must also know the Bible very well, know spiritual needs, and be able to apply the Bible's teachings to daily living.

4. The church should never use this process as a way to approve everyone who wants to be **ordained**. The normal way to become a minister of the Word is through training at **Calvin Theological Seminary**.

*Special Advice to Classis Red Mesa*

1. The process for Native Americans to be ordained in Classis Red Mesa is this:

- The normal way to become a minister is to study at Calvin Seminary and to complete all the usual requirements for **ordination**.
- If a person cannot go to the seminary, he may be ordained by way of this special process if he has exceptional gifts. The person must apply to his church council—or to Classis Red Mesa, if there is no council.

—see Church Order, Art. 7; Supplement, Art. 7

**Ministers Who May Receive a Call**

A minister of the Word in the CRC may be called by a local church, in line with rules set up by synod.

A minister from another **denomination** may want to become a minister in the CRC. In order to be called by a local church, he needs to be examined by the **classis** of that church. The exam will deal with his training in theology and how well he did as a minister where he served before. The exam will also deal with his understanding of Reformed teachings. The minister also needs to show that he is a godly Christian leader. The **synodical deputies** need to be present at the exam. They sometimes give advice to the classis in making a decision. The deputies and the classis must agree before the decision is final. If they both approve the minister, the classis may declare that he is ready for a call.

A local church may want to call a minister from another denomination. But it may not do that unless the classis approves him and says he may be called. All this must be done in line with the rules set up by synod.

*(A minister may leave the CRC to become a minister in another denomination. If a minister has done that, and he wants to become a CRC minister again, he must return by way of Article 8 of the Church Order—not Article 14. See Church Order, Art. 8, 14.)*

*Nominating a Minister Who Has Served His Church Less than Two Years*

When a church is without a **pastor,** it may nominate ministers that it wants to call. The classis assigns a counselor to help the church as it looks for a new minister. A **council** should not usually nominate a minister who has served less than two years in his present church. But there may be special and serious reasons to nominate a certain minister who has been at his church for less than two years. If the counselor agrees, then the council may go ahead and nominate the minister. The counselor must explain to the classis why he agreed to this action.

*Calling the Same Minister within a Year*

A church may not call the same minister twice in the same year unless the classis says it may do so.

*Calling a Minister to Serve for a Certain Period of Time*

1. Sometimes a church wants to call a minister for a certain period of time. If a church makes a call like that, then the letter of call must explain two things. It must explain how the church would reappoint the minister later, when the time period was up. The letter must also explain how the church would help him financially if he was not reappointed.

2. The church's **counselor** must make sure that these two items in the letter of call are fair and reasonable.

3. If the church does not reappoint the minister when the time is up, he becomes available for call for the next two years. If the minister does not receive a call in that time, the classis and the synodical deputies must declare that he is no longer a minister. But if they have good reasons, they may decide to keep him available for call for a year at a time.

*Calling Ministers from Other Denominations*

1. Normally only ministers of the CRC may be called to serve in the churches. But in some cases a church may call someone from another denomination. A church may do that only after it has done all it can to call a minister of the CRC.

2. If a minister from another denomination wants to serve in the CRC, he must apply to the classis where he wants to serve. Or he must apply to the classis that is closest to the area he wants to serve in.

3. The synodical deputies must be sure that there is a *need* for this minister to come into the CRC. Before they talk about the need, the minister must show the classis a statement of health, his diplomas, and a report of his mental health. The deputies must give their approval of the need at a classis meeting. They must also give their approval of the need at a later meeting of classis, when the minister will be examined. The classis must put an announcement in *The Banner* about the need for this minister and about his future examination. (*The Banner* is the weekly magazine of the Christian Reformed Church.)

4. A council may not nominate a minister from another denomination unless the classis approves him for a call. The classis and the synodical deputies must examine him to approve him. **Classis** will schedule the exam after making sure that he needs to be called. (The exam is called a *colloquium doctum,* or "doctrinal conversation.") Classis may do this in agreement with the synodical deputies. A written report about the need will be part of the deputies' report to the next year's synod.

5. The need for calling a minister from another denomination will be based on one of these reasons:

   • He has such exceptional gifts that the local church feels it is important for the CRC to have him as a minister.
   • The local church has such a great need for a minister that it must call one from outside the CRC.

6. The classis will write the report about the need for calling this minister or making him available for call (see point 4 above). The **synodical deputies** must agree with this report before classis examines the minister.

7. Classis and the synodical deputies must be open to looking into the need in this situation. At the same time, they must follow synod's rules about calling a minister from outside the CRC.

8. At the exam (the *colloquium doctum),* the minister will present a statement about his beliefs and Christian walk. This statement is to be written by the council or classis (or **presbytery**) of his own church.

   (Now, the minister may come from a church that does not accept the teachings of the Reformed faith. If that is the case, it may find him unacceptable—just because he agrees with the Reformed faith. As a result, that church may not want to write a statement about him. Then the classis and the synodical deputies will have to make a careful investigation into his beliefs and Christian walk. They should write a report about this investigation. If they are satisfied with him, their report may serve as the statement about his beliefs and Christian walk.)

9. The classis and synodical deputies will approve or not approve the minister by examining

- his beliefs,
- his Christian walk, and
- his knowledge and appreciation of how things work in the CRC.

10. When a minister from another country is examined, the synodical deputies must make sure that he

- can speak or learn English,
- can adjust to the American or Canadian lifestyle, and
- is less than 40 years old (in general).

11. The minister must pass the examination (*colloquium doctum*) and be approved by the synodical deputies. After that, the classis may declare that he is available for call in the CRC. No further exam is needed.

*Deciding Need*

1. When a **council** or classis wants to call a minister from outside the CRC, the synodical deputies must make sure that there is indeed a "need." This is also true when a minister from another denomination wants to become a minister in the CRC.

2. The council or classis must present written information to the synodical deputies about this "need." If the deputies approve of this written information, it will become part of their report at the next year's synod.

—see Church Order, Art. 8; Supplement, Art. 8

**The Role of a Counselor**

When a local church is without a minister, the classis assigns a **counselor** to help the council as it looks for another minister. The counselor's job is to make sure that all church rules are followed in the process. Both the council and the counselor sign the letter of call. At the next meeting of classis, the counselor must report on his work with the local church.

—see Church Order, Art. 9

**Ordaining and Installing**

When a council calls a **candidate**—a graduate of seminary who has not served before as a minister—he has to be **ordained** as a minister of the Word. Before he can be ordained, the candidate has to be approved by the classis and the synodical deputies. So the classis examines the candidate in terms of his beliefs and his Christian walk, in line with rules set by synod. The synodical deputies must be present for this exam.

The candidate will be ordained during a worship service. When the candidate is being ordained, the minister in charge of the worship service will lay hands on him.

When a council calls a minister who is already ordained, he has to be approved by the classis before he can be **installed** as the church's minister. He must give written statements to the classis (or its **interim committee**) from his former council and classis. These statements are about his beliefs and his Christian walk. When he is approved, he will be installed during a worship service.

*Rules about Candidates*

1. The letter of call sent to a candidate must say that the classis has to examine the candidate before he can be ordained.

2. Once the candidate has passed the exam and has been approved by classis, the date of his ordination may be announced.

3. The candidate has to preach a sermon on a Bible text chosen by the classis. The preaching will take place during a regular worship service while members of the classis are there. This is usually done in the church that has called the candidate. It is also usually done on the Sunday before the next meeting of classis.

4. Classis will get a copy of the sermon from the candidate. Then, before the classis meeting, copies will go to the synodical deputies and to the **delegates** of classis.

5. The candidate will also give copies of two other sermons to the **classis**. These are to be sermons that he has preached as a student. One of these two sermons will be based on a Scripture text. The other sermon will be based on a Lord's Day of the **Heidelberg Catechism**. The Scripture texts used in the two sermons should come from the Old and New Testaments. These sermons may not be ones that the student wrote for classwork or for practice preaching at the seminary.

6. When **synod** declares someone a candidate, that means the person has met all the academic requirements for being a candidate. It also means that he is in good health and that he has been recommended by a **council**. So classis normally does not need to ask questions about these areas when it examines a candidate.

7. Classis will appoint four of its **delegates** to be the official examiners. Two will evaluate the sermons and will be at the worship service where the candidate preaches. The other two will conduct the exam at the meeting of classis.

8. Synod has set the following schedule for the examination by classis:

   a. *Introduction*
   One of the examiners will introduce the candidate to the classis.

   b. *Exam*

      1) *Practice (practica)* (no time limit)

         a) The examiner will ask the candidate about his relationship with God and about his commitment to being a minister. The examiner will ask what the candidate understands about the meaning and value of ministry today. The examiner will ask the candidate if he is loyal to the CRC. Questions related to these things may also be asked.

b) The **synodical deputies** and delegates may ask additional questions.

c) A motion must be made and passed before the next part of the exam may begin.

2) *Sermon Evaluation*

a) In the presence of the candidate, the written sermons are evaluated. The examiners also evaluate how the candidate did as he preached in the worship service.

b) The synodical deputies and delegates may ask additional questions about the sermons. They may also ask about the delivery during the worship service.

c) Again, a motion must be made and passed to begin the next part of the exam. The synodical deputies must be in favor of this motion before it can pass.

3) *Biblical and Theological Position* (at least 30 minutes for each candidate)

a) The examiner will ask questions to see how much the candidate knows about the Bible and theology, how deep his understanding is, and how accurate his views are.

b) The synodical deputies and delegates may ask additional questions (no exact time limit).

c. *Process for Being Admitted to the Ministry*

1) The classis will go into executive session. That means only the voting delegates may remain in the room. During that time, a motion is made to admit the candidate to ministry in the CRC.

2) The classis prays, asking for the guidance of the Holy Spirit.

3) The synodical deputies leave the room to prepare their recommendation to the classis.

4) Meanwhile, the classis votes by ballot to approve or not to approve the candidate.

5) The synodical deputies come back and read their written statement. When they do this, it becomes clear whether or not they agree with the vote of classis.

6) If the classis and synodical deputies do not agree, they may try to reach a decision they can both agree on.

7) If they cannot agree, then the matter is passed along to synod for a decision.

—see Church Order, Art. 10; Supplement, Art. 10

## The Role of the Minister of the Word

The calling of a minister of the Word is a calling from God and from the church. A minister preaches the Word of God. This means he proclaims the truths of the Bible. It also means he explains what the Bible says and how we should apply it to our lives. The purpose of his calling is to bring together God's people as the church of Jesus Christ and to help them grow as members of the church.

—see Church Order, Art. 11

### The Work and Calling of Ministers of the Word

A minister of the Word may serve as a pastor in a local church. He preaches the Word of God and leads the worship services. He also does **baptism** and leads the church in the **Lord's Supper**. He teaches the young people the truths of the Bible by means of the **catechism**. He also trains the members of the church to live in Christian service to God and all people.

The minister and the **elders** are in charge of correction and **discipline** for all church members, including those who are in the council. The minister and the elders must also make sure everything in the church is done in a decent and orderly way. The minister and the elders share the work of pastoral care in the congregation. They also **evangelize** and teach others to evangelize.

A minister of the Word may also serve as a **missionary**—either in North America or in a foreign country. And sometimes synod may appoint a minister to a specific job—in a college, on a CRC board, in a **CRC agency**, or as a **chaplain**. In any of these cases, the minister must be called by a local church before he can begin his work. The local church calls him in the same way it calls a pastor. Then he is appointed to do the work he has been called to do. All this is done in cooperation with classis and synod.

A minister of the Word may also do other work that fits with his calling as a minister. He must be called by a local church before he can begin this work. The church may call him only after **classis** and the **synodical deputies** agree that this work fits with his calling as a minister of the Word.

*Rules about Specific Tasks and Situations of Ministers*

1. Before a church calls a minister for a specific task, the task must be approved by the classis and the synodical deputies. The church will give classis the following information:

   a. A description of the position to be filled (purposes, duties, requirements, and so on), in line with the rules of any agency that is involved.

   b. Proof that the minister will be supervised by the church. This proof will include an outline that tells the minister how he should report to the church. It also will state how the minister will be supervised, in line with the rules of any agency that is involved.

   c. A statement that shows how the task fits in with the minister's calling as a minister of the Word.

   d. *Special case:* A position to be filled may be one that was called "spiritual in character and directly related to the ministerial calling" before June 1978. If it was, then classis and the synodical deputies will review the position again. They need to make sure it agrees with Articles 11-14 of the Church Order (see Church Order, Art. 11-14).

2. Sometimes a new ministry calls for quick action. In a case like that, the calling church (and the agency that is involved) may be able to get "provisional approval" to begin the new ministry. This kind of approval

may be given by the **interim committee** of classis. This approval has to be supported by classis later. At the next classis meeting, the classis and the synodical deputies have to decide whether or not to approve the new ministry.

If they do not approve the ministry, the minister may still want to continue in the work he has started. If he does, he may be honorably released from the ministry in the CRC. Then later he may be accepted back into the ministry in the CRC, in line with the rules of Church Order (see Church Order, Art. 14-c and -d.)

3. A minister may be called to be a chaplain in the military or in an institution (like a hospital, prison, university, or business corporation). Before calling a minister to be a chaplain, the calling church should ask the Chaplain Committee of the CRC to approve him.

4. Each year, the **church visitors** from classis will ask the calling church about the minister who has been called to a specific task. They will ask how the minister is being supervised. They will also ask how the minister is reporting about his work. The church visitors will let the classis know if the church or the minister is not living up to the agreement made earlier. This agreement has to do with supervising and reporting (see point 1 above).

—see Church Order, Art. 12; Supplement, Art. 12-c

## Supervision of Ministers

A minister of the Word is supervised by the church that calls him. This church supervises his preaching and teaching. It also supervises his Christian walk and his work as a pastor. If his work is with another church (or workplace), the supervision is shared with that church (or workplace; see also "The Work and Calling of Ministers of the Word" above).

A minister of the Word may be loaned for a time to be a pastor in a church outside the CRC. His calling church does the loaning. The classis and the synodical deputies need to approve the loan before it takes place. This loan must be in line with the rules set up by synod. The calling church will supervise the minister in terms of his beliefs and his Christian walk. His calling church may also work with the other church to decide what his work will be.

*Rules about Ministers on Loan*

When a minister is on loan to a church outside the CRC, he may still keep his status as a minister in the CRC. This is possible under the following conditions:

1. The church is interested in the Reformed faith and is thinking seriously about becoming part of the CRC or part of another Reformed **denomination**. Or the congregation may already be Reformed and may want to grow in the Reformed faith.

2. If the church is not a Reformed church already, the minister sees it as his duty to help that church come into the CRC or into another Reformed body of believers.

3. The work of the minister is to be spiritual in nature and directly related to his calling as a minister. This work may not go against his promise to

serve the CRC faithfully. His work must be in line with the Form of Subscription (see "Signing the Form of Subscription," p. 12).

4. If the church is near a CRC church in another classis, the loan needs to be approved by that classis and by the synodical deputies. It also needs to be approved by the classis of the calling church.

5. The minister may be on loan for two years. Classis and the synodical deputies may extend the loan for two years at a time, if needed.

6. If the minister needs to be disciplined, the non-CRC church may **suspend** him from his work there. But only the CRC will have the right to suspend him from the office of minister. And only the CRC may **depose** him from that office, if necessary.

7. If the minister wants to stay on the CRC Pension Plan, he or the church he is serving must make payments into the Plan. The amount for ministers working outside the CRC is set yearly by the Minister's Pension Fund Committee.

—see Church Order, Art. 13; Supplement, Art. 13-b

### Release from the Office of Minister

If a minister wants to leave his local church to work in another church, he must have the permission of his **council**.

A minister of the Word may resign from the CRC to work in ministry outside the CRC. The **classis** will release him from office and will declare what his status is. The classis may do this in agreement with the **synodical deputies**.

A minister of the Word may not leave the ministry whenever he wants to. But he may be released from office to do non-pastoral work. This kind of release needs to be approved by classis and the synodical deputies. And there must be strong reasons for doing it.

When a minister has worked in a non-pastoral job for one year, then he may be released from office. The classis may do this in agreement with the synodical deputies.

A minister who has been released from office may become a minister again. The classis that released him may declare him ready for a call. The classis may do this if the synodical deputies agree. If a church calls him to be their pastor, the minister also needs to be **ordained** again.

*(If a minister resigned to become a minister in another denomination, he may come back into the CRC by way of Article 8 of the Church Order. See Church Order, Art. 8)*

*About Ministers Who Resign from the CRC*

1. If a minister resigns to look for work as a minister outside the CRC, his church and classis need to decide how they will discharge him. They may do this in agreement with the synodical deputies. Synod notes that this advice gives a lot of room for handling this kind of situation in different ways.

2. As they decide on what to do, the church and the classis need to think carefully about how the minister acted before he resigned. They may also need to look at how he acted *when* he resigned. (In some situations the

church may consider that he may be **deposed**. Other situations may call for a simple release from office.)

3. The church and classis need to take note of all details that may enter into the case. (For example, the minister may resign in a formal way, or he might just leave without a warning.) The church and classis need to state how he acted and what his status is. Their statement could show one of the following:

   - The resigned minister is honorably released.
   - The resigned minister is released.
   - The resigned minister is dismissed.
   - The resigned minister is considered as one who has been deposed.

*Note: A resigned minister no longer has the honor and title of minister of the Word in the CRC. He no longer has credentials in the CRC. (He may not be allowed to have the status of a retired minister. See Church Order, Article 18-b.)*

4. As they try to make a decision, the church and the classis should ask the Lord to guide them, especially as they think about these points:

   - If a minister does things that divide or break down the church, he makes a serious mistake. He violates the sacred trust connected with ordination. He also dishonors the Lord, whose body is the church.
   - It is possible that the minister who resigned can be restored. It's also possible that he and the church can work together again in Christian love. Any statement about a resigned minister should show that there's still hope for these things to happen.

—see Church Order, Art. 14; Supplement, Art. 14-b

**Support of Ministers**

The local church is responsible to support its pastor financially. When a church cannot do that, the pastor may be allowed to find work outside the ministry to help support himself. This action needs to be approved by the classis. This is usually done only when the local church cannot get enough help to support its minister.

*Rules for a Church Whose Minister Has to Find Work Outside the Ministry*

1. The local church must at least support its minister in terms of the number of hours he spends in ministry each week. (Full-time work is 48 hours a week.) The financial support normally includes a minimum salary, housing costs, and other benefits (insurance, pension, vacation, and so on). The salary must be at least the minimum amount set by the **Fund for Smaller Churches**.

2. The financial support includes money to be used for health insurance. The minister is to find good health insurance for himself and his family.

3. If the church has a parsonage, the value of it may be used toward the financial support of the minister.

4. The minister receives pension credits in the **Ministers' Pension Fund**. The amount of credit he gets depends on the amount of time he spends

working for the church. He may have full pension credit if full contribution for him is made to the pension plan.

5. The kind of work the minister will be doing outside of ministry must be clearly understood. The same goes for the amount of time he will spend at this work. A minister should not have to work more than 60 hours a week (average) in his work for the church and outside the church.

—see Church Order, Art. 15; Supplement, Art. 15

## Release from Service in a Congregation

*Leave of Absence.* Sometimes the minister feels he needs to get away from the work of the local church for a while. If the **council** agrees that he has good reasons for doing this, it may give him a leave of absence. While he is on leave, the council must still supervise him in terms of his Christian walk.

*Initiated by the Minister.* Sometimes a minister feels he can no longer work for the local church he is serving. He must have good reasons for doing this. If his council and classis approve, they can release him from his work for that church. But the church must still help to provide for him. The council will set up a plan that says how much and how long it will help him. This plan needs to be approved by classis.

When a minister has been released from his work in a local church, he may be called by another congregation. If he does not get a call within two years, the classis must declare that he is no longer a minister. The classis may do this in agreement with the **synodical deputies**. But if they have good reasons, the classis and the deputies may keep him available for call for a year at a time.

If a minister has been released in this way, he may have his credentials transferred to the church where he is a member. This transfer needs to be approved by classis. The classis also has to say when the transfer will take place.

—see Church Order, Art. 16; Supplement, Art. 16-b and -c

## Release from Ministry in a Congregation

*Initiated by the Council.* Sometimes a **council** feels that it should release a minister from his work. The council may want this even though the minister has been faithful in his work and in his Christian walk. It may want this even though he is not ready or able to retire. The council must have good reasons for wanting him released. If the **classis** and the synodical deputies agree with these reasons, he may be released. All this must be done in line with rules set up by synod.

If the minister is released, the council must still help to provide for him. The council will set up a plan that says how much and how long it will help him. This plan needs to be approved by classis.

When the minister has been released, he may be called by another local church. If he does not get a call within two years, the classis must declare that he is no longer a minister. Classis may do this in agreement with the synodical deputies. But if they have good reasons, classis and the deputies may keep the minister available for call for a year at a time.

If a minister has been released by way of this process and has transferred his membership to another local church, he may have his credentials transferred to the church where he is a member. This transfer needs to be approved by classis. The classis will say when the transfer will take place.

—see Church Order, Art. 17; Supplement, Art. 17

## Retirement of Ministers

A minister may retire from office for any one of these reasons:

- He has reached retirement age.
- He has a physical disability and cannot do his work.
- He has a mental disability and cannot do his work.

The minister may do this if the council and classis approve, in line with rules set up by synod.

If a minister is retired, he is still worthy of being called a minister of the Word. His credentials will stay at the church he retired from. That church is to provide properly for him and his household, in line with rules set up by synod.

A minister may come out of retirement if he does not need to be retired anymore. He needs to ask the council and classis that retired him to make him available for call again.

*Retirement Options*

- Ministers who serve as professors at **Calvin College** or at **Calvin Theological Seminary** may retire at age 65, if they want to. They may retire with full retirement benefits.
- A minister of the Word may retire at age 55, if the classis approves this action. His pension will be in line with the reduced pension scale adopted by Synod 1978.
- If a retired minister moves his membership to another church in the CRC, he may want to move his credentials and support there too. The minister has to ask for this transfer. (If he stays as a member of the church he retired from, there is no transfer. If he does not expect to stay retired, there is no transfer.) The council of the church he retired from must ask the council of the other church to accept the credentials and support of this minister.

—see Church Order, Art. 18; Supplement, Art. 18

## Theological Seminary

The churches of the CRC must provide for a seminary where its ministers are trained. Synod governs this official seminary—**Calvin Theological Seminary**—by means of a **board of trustees**. This board is appointed by synod and is responsible to synod for what it does.

—see Church Order, Art. 19

## Tasks of Professors of Theology

The **professors** of theology at the seminary must be ministers of the Word. Their job is to train students for the ministry of the Word. They must also train the students to preach the Word and to defend the Christian faith against false teachings.

—see Church Order, Art. 20

## Student Fund

The local churches are to look for persons who could become ministers of the Word. Church members must encourage these persons to go to seminary. The churches must provide funds if a student needs help with the cost of going to seminary. Every classis needs to have a student fund for this purpose.

—see Church Order, Art. 21

## Licensing of Students

A student in the seminary may be licensed to lead a worship service, in line with rules set by synod. This means he may explain **(exhort)** the Word of God during the worship service.

*Rules for Licensing*

1.  The Board of Trustees of Calvin Theological Seminary may give a license for leading worship services in the CRC to a person who

    - is a regular student in the seminary, and
    - has passed the final exam for the junior year at the seminary.

2.  The board may not give a license to a student until it is sure that

    - he is a **confessing adult member** in **good standing** in the CRC.
    - he has spiritual gifts needed for ministry. The student must also believe he is called by God to prepare for becoming a minister.
    - he plans to enter the CRC ministry when he graduates.
    - he has a deep knowledge of the Bible and the Reformed teachings so that he can be a guide to others.
    - he speaks well and builds up his listeners in the faith. To get this information, the board may check with the professors at the seminary, or it may examine the student.

3.  A student may want to take postgraduate studies. If so, the board may extend his license. But it may do that only under these conditions:

    - The student must be taking postgraduate work in theology. The student has to declare that he fully intends to serve as a minister in the CRC.
    - The extension may last for only one year.
    - At the end of the first year, the student may be given another year if he puts his request in writing. Then, if he wants another year, he must come to the board in person and be willing to take another exam. (If the student is studying outside the U.S. or Canada, he does not have to come in person.)

4.  The board will have to take away the license

    - if the student has completed his studies but has not begun the process to become a minister of the Word.
    - if the student has quit his studies or has not enrolled again at the seminary.

*Rules for Licensing Students from Foreign Countries*

1. The student must be a confessing adult member of a faithful Reformed Church. He must also be a regular or special student at the seminary.

2. The student must have enough training at the seminary for the professors to recommend him. He must also be able to speak English well.

3. The student must have passed a course in homiletics (the art of preaching) at the seminary or at another school. He must show the professor of homiletics that he can **exhort** well.

4. The student's request for a license must be sent to the secretary of the board of trustees.

5. The board or its executive committee must interview the student.

6. Any preaching (exhorting) that the student does must be arranged by the seminary.

7. The student's license will be good as long as he stays at the seminary. The board may extend his license only in a special situation.

*Licensing of Students from Non-Anglo Groups*

Some cultures have a tradition of **ordaining** the student early, before he finishes his training in theology. (For example, the African and Hispanic cultures tend to do that.) A student from a culture with that tradition must finish one-half of the M.Min. degree to get a license. This license allows him to do all of the usual pastoral duties. This means he may also do **baptism** and lead the church in the **Lord's Supper**. The council must supervise all of these activities. The license may be renewed by classis while the student continues his work on the M.Min. degree. His studies will eventually lead to his ordination as a minister of the Word. (*Note:* Calvin Theological Seminary recently discontinued the M.Min. program in favor of an adjusted M.Div. program.)

—see Church Order, Art. 22; Supplement, Art. 22

### C. Evangelists

**The Office of Evangelist**

An **evangelist** is called to help a group of believers become a church. He is an **elder** of the church that has called him to this work. He has the same privileges and responsibilities as any other elder. But his work is usually limited to the work of an evangelist.

The evangelist's work in a group of believers usually ends when the group becomes an **organized church**. But sometimes it is wise for him to keep working with the group after it becomes an organized church. He may do this if the new church's council and the classis approve. Then the evangelist may stay until the church has an ordained minister. Or he may stay until a reasonable amount of time has passed and the church can act on its own.

An evangelist may also serve an organized church along with a minister of the Word.

An evangelist may do work that is not part of his job as an evangelist. Before he begins any work like this, it must be approved by the consistory (elders) and the classis.

*Requirements*

Before a person is ordained as an evangelist in the CRC, he must prove that he can work well in evangelism. He must also pass an exam before classis. The exam includes these items:

1. Presenting the following documents:

   - a recommendation from his church council
   - proof of general education (diplomas, transcripts, and so on) and proof of special training in theology and evangelism
   - a copy of the letter from the church that wants to ordain him as an evangelist (this is called the letter of appointment)
   - a copy of the letter he wrote to accept the offer (this is called the letter of acceptance)

2. Preaching a sermon:

   - The person must preach a sermon on a text assigned by classis. This will take place in an official worship service. If possible, this will also take place on the Sunday before the meeting of classis. If possible, this will also take place in the church that is calling him to be an evangelist. Two members of the classis must be present to serve as sermon critics.
   - Copies of the sermon will be given to the **delegates** at the classis meeting. The sermon critics will evaluate the sermon. They will also evaluate how well he led the worship service. The person will be present during this part of the exam.

3. Testing in these areas:

   - Bible knowledge
   - knowledge of Reformed teachings
   - knowledge of the **creeds** and **confessions** and the Church Order of the CRC
   - Christian-life issues—Christian walk, relationships with other people, love for the church, interest in evangelism, promoting the kingdom of God

When an evangelist accepts a call to another location, his ordination needs to be approved by the classis there. He has to be recommended by the council and classis that he last served. They are to write up a statement about his beliefs and his Christian walk. He must give this statement to the classis of the calling church, for their approval.

—see Church Order, Art. 23; Supplement, Art. 23-b

**Ministry of Evangelists**

The work of the evangelist is to be a witness for Christ, discipling the lost. The evangelist does this by preaching the Word, baptizing, leading the church in the Lord's Supper, and doing evangelism. He also does this by inviting young people and adults to grow in their faith through church education. He also provides pastoral care. He does all of this to build up the church and to bring unbelievers to Jesus Christ. The evangelist must also teach fellow believers how to bring the good news of Jesus to other people.

The evangelist is supervised by the council of his calling church. He must give regular reports to the council. He should go to the meetings of council whenever he can, especially when council is going to talk about his work.

—see Church Order, Art. 24

## D. Elders and Deacons

**Ministry of Elders and Deacons**

The **elders** and **deacons** serve in the local church. They serve for a limited time. The council decides how long their term of office is. The council also decides how many elders and deacons will finish their terms each year. This is done so that there are always trained elders and deacons in the council when new ones come in each year. Elders and deacons who have finished their terms are not usually elected again right away. But the church may decide that it still needs them. If the elders and deacons are elected again, they need to be **installed** again.

The elders, along with the minister (or ministers), are responsible for all the members of the local church, including the members of the council. The elders oversee the spiritual life of the members. They help the members to understand the Bible. They correct and **discipline** the members, if necessary. They provide pastoral care for the members. They **evangelize**, and they encourage others to share the good news of Jesus with other people. The elders must also defend the faith.

The deacons are to bring the mercy of Christ to all people. They must try to help all people in need, especially those who are part of the local church. The deacons are to encourage the church members to give their money, time, and talents to help people in need. The deacons must do all this to help the church see that Christ has called them to a ministry of the Word and of deeds.

—see Church Order, Art. 25; see also
"The Mission of the Congregation," p. 47

# Part 2: The Assemblies of the Church

## A. General Information

### Assemblies of the Church

The assemblies of the church are the **council**, the **classis**, and the **synod**. (The classis is made up of several local churches in an area. The synod is a meeting of people sent by all the classes.)

—see Church Order, Art. 26

### Authority of Church Assemblies

Jesus Christ has given the church its authority. Each assembly is an extension of the church. So each assembly has authority given by Christ.

The council's authority is called *original* authority. This means that the authority to build up the church begins with the council, under Christ. The council builds up the local church as the body of Christ. It does this by calling the local church to serve and to honor Christ. (See also "Congregational Meetings," p. 35.)

The authority of classis and synod is called *delegated* authority. Each council sends **delegates** to classis. And each classis sends delegates to synod. The purpose of sending delegates in this way is to unite the churches, to resolve difficult issues, and to do ministry together that no one church can do alone.

A local church agrees to listen to the common voice of the other churches in the classis. So in this way the classis has authority over the council.

The classis also agrees to listen to the decisions of synod. So in this way synod has authority over the classis.

The classis has the same authority over the council as the synod has over the classis.

—see Church Order, Art. 27

### Matters That the Assemblies Deal With

The assemblies of the church (council, classis, synod) deal only with church matters. They make their decisions in a decent and orderly way, in line with the teachings of the Bible.

A classis or a synod deals only with two kinds of issues:

- Issues that affect the churches it works with. In other words, when a classis meets, it deals with issues that affect *its own churches*. When synod meets, it deals with issues that affect *all the churches*.
- Issues that could not be finished in a council or classis.

Issues that go to classis or synod need to go by the rules set up for classis and synod.

For information about taking issues to synod, see Part V of the Rules for Synodical Procedure. These rules are updated each year along with the Church Order. They are published by the office of the CRC **general secretary** in the book *Church Order/Rules for Synodical Procedure*.

—see Church Order, Art. 28; Supplement, Art. 28

## Nature of Assembly Decisions

The assemblies of the church (council, classis, synod) need to make their decisions carefully. They need to pray that the Lord will guide them. They need to think carefully and try to obey the Word of God as they decide. They need to take time to discuss issues that are important to the church.

When they make a decision, it is "settled and binding." This means that all the churches involved need to go along with it. The decision may not be changed unless someone proves that it goes against the Bible or the Church Order.

—see Church Order, Art. 29

## Appeals

A person or an assembly may ask to have a decision changed. They must have good reasons for doing this. They may feel that the decision is unjust. They may feel that it goes against the Bible or the Church Order. All appeals must follow the rules set up for making appeals.

For example, a person may appeal to classis to change a decision. If the classis does not change it, the person may then go a step further and appeal to synod. A classis may also make an appeal to synod.

Synod may decide how to deal with appeals.

Synod uses a set of rules for dealing with appeals. This set of rules includes a judicial code.

—see Church Order, Art. 30; Supplement, Art. 30-a, -b, -c

## Request to Change a Decision

If you want a decision changed, you have to ask the assembly that made the decision. That assembly will decide whether or not to deal with the request. It will deal with the request if it feels that you have good reasons or new grounds for change.

A request to change a decision of classis must first go through the council. A request to change a decision of synod must first go through the council and then through the classis.

—see Church Order, Art. 31; Supplement, Art. 31

## How Assemblies Are Run

All meetings of assemblies (council, classis, synod) are to begin with prayer. They are also to end with prayer.

Every assembly will have a president. This person will make sure everyone understands the issues to be dealt with at the meeting. He will make sure that the rules of Church Order are followed. He will also see that the meeting is conducted decently and in order.

Every assembly will also have a clerk. This person will take notes on what happens at the meeting.

In a meeting of classis or synod, the president and clerk will serve only during the meeting. They will no longer be president and clerk after the meeting. At the next meeting of classis or synod, a new president and a new clerk will be elected.

Each assembly will decide how it will receive information, appeals, or proposals. It will also prepare an agenda, a list of what it wants to do at the meeting. The assembly will keep clear records of the meetings. The records will be kept in files for use in the future. The assembly will also decide how to handle its financial matters.

If the assembly owns property, it must be legally recorded under the legal name of the assembly. The assembly must be registered with the government with the right to hold property. This may be at the local, state (or provincial), or federal government level.

—see Church Order, Art. 32

## Assembly Committees

The assemblies may set up committees to make sure their decisions are carried out. They may also set up committees to study issues that need to be decided on. The committees need to know exactly what they are expected to do. They also need to give regular reports on the work they are doing.

Each classis will set up a classical **interim committee**. Each synod will set up a synodical interim committee. These committees will deal with issues that come up when classis or synod are not meeting. Sometimes an issue cannot wait until the next meeting of classis or synod. If that is the case, then the interim committee may make a decision on that issue. Each interim committee needs to know exactly what it is expected to do. It needs to bring a report of all its actions to the next meeting of the classis or synod. This report needs to be approved by the classis or synod.

—see Church Order, Art. 33

## Delegates at Assemblies

Each council sends **delegates** to classis meetings. Each classis sends delegates to synod. The delegates are **elders** and **ministers**. Each delegate will be sent with a document (credentials) showing that he may speak for the council or classis. As a delegate, he may also vote on behalf of his council or classis. The delegate may not vote on any issue that deals with himself or his church in particular.

—see Church Order, Art. 34

## B. The Council

## Makeup of a Council

A local church is led by a council. The council is made up of the minister, elders, and **deacons**. Sometimes there is more than one minister. The council makes decisions about things that affect everyone in the church. For example, the council sends out the call for a pastor. The council approves the church members who can be elected to office.

The members of council also practice **mutual censure** (see "Council Meetings and Mutual Censure" below).

The council also meets with the **church visitors**. These are visitors from the classis. They make a visit to each local church once a year to see how things are going in the church.

The council is made up of two parts. One part is the **consistory**. The minister (or ministers) and the elders make up the consistory. All the tasks of the elders are the responsibility of the consistory.

The other part of the council is the **diaconate**. This part is made up of the deacons. It is responsible for all the work of the deacons. They take charge of the ministry of mercy to people in need. The deacons must report to the rest of the council on the work they do.

(See also "Ministry of Elders and Deacons," p. 30.)

The council is to prepare the yearly budget for the local church. This budget should include the **ministry shares** for the classis and for the **CRC agencies** set up by synod. The budget needs to be approved by the congregation.

—see Church Order, Art. 35; Supplement, Art. 35-a

## Council Meetings and Mutual Censure

The council meets at least once a month. The consistory (elders) also holds a separate meeting once a month. So does the diaconate. They let the church members know when they will meet, in case anyone wants to present something to them.

Usually the minister is the president of the council and the consistory. He leads the meetings of these groups.

A council may choose to elect an elder as its president. This often happens in a church that has two ministers (or more). It will also happen if the church is without a minister.

The deacons elect one of their members to be the president of the diaconate.

At least four times a year the council must practice **mutual censure**. This deals with how well the minister, elders, and deacons are doing their work. They do this to build each other up, to discuss any problems they may have with each other, and to pray for the Lord's healing and help in their work together for the local church.

—see Church Order, Art. 36

## Congregational Meetings

The council needs the advice of the local church when it makes major decisions. For example, the council asks the church to help when it is time to choose new elders and deacons.

The council does not ask for advice on matters of supervision or **discipline**. These matters are the task of the council only.

To get the advice of the congregation, the council needs to call a congregational meeting. This should be done at least once a year. Any member of the local church may go to this meeting. But only the **confessing adult members** in **good standing** may vote.

The council leads the congregational meeting. The people will talk only about the issues brought up by the council. The council will take in all the advice of the church members at this meeting. But the final decision is the council's. The council was elected to supervise and govern. So it has the final word on the decisions it makes for the local church.

—see Church Order, Art. 37

## Before a Council Is Set Up

If a group of believers does not have a council yet, it will be cared for and supervised by the council of a nearby church. The classis will assign this work to that council.

When a group is ready to set up its council for the first time, this action needs to be approved by the classis.

—see Church Order, Art. 38

## C. The Classis

## Makeup of a Classis

A classis is made up of CRC churches in a certain area. The synod decides what churches belong to a classis.

The classis needs to collect funds for the work of classis and the **denomination**. It must also distribute those funds where they need to go. This task is the job of the treasurer of classis. This work should be done in such a way that the richer churches help out the poorer ones.

—see Church Order, Art. 39; Supplement, Art. 39

## Meetings of Classis

The council of each local church sends two **delegates** to the meetings of classis. These delegates should be a **minister** and an **elder**. If the church does not have a minister, the council may send two elders instead. The council may also do this if the minister cannot go to the meeting.

Other elders and **deacons** may go to the meeting, but they may not be official delegates. They may give advice at the meeting, but they may not vote.

Classis normally meets three times a year (every four months). But if a classis covers a large area, it may not be able to meet that often. The meeting is held at the time and place that were agreed on at the last meeting.

Normally a minister will serve as the president of a classis meeting. The ministers of the classis may take turns doing this. Or the classis may elect one of the delegates to be president. The same person may not be president at two meetings in a row.

### Exception for Classis Red Mesa

The council sends *three* delegates to the classis meeting. These delegates should be a minister and *two* elders. If the church does not have a minister, it will send *three* elders. The council may also do this if the minister cannot go to the meeting.

Other elders and deacons may go to the meeting, but they may not be official delegates. They may give advice at the meeting, but they may not vote.

The classis will elect one of the delegates to be president at the meeting. The same person may not be elected twice in a row.

—see Church Order, Art. 40; Supplement, Art. 40-a and -c

## Questions to Each Council at Classis

When classis meets, the president of classis will ask a series of questions on behalf of the classis. These questions are for the delegates of each church to answer:

1. Does the council meet regularly in your church (minister, elders, deacons together)? Does the consistory (minister and elders)? Do the deacons? Are the needs of the church members dealt with in those meetings?

2. Do you practice church **discipline** faithfully?

3. Do the deacons take care of people in need? Do they encourage the church members to give of their money, time, and talents to people in need?

4. Does the council talk to church members about Christian education? Does the council tell them how important that is from kindergarten through college?

5. a. Since the last meeting of classis, have any church members moved to a town where there is no CRC? If so, have you reported their new addresses to CRC Home Missions?

   b. Have any members moved to an area where there is a CRC? This also applies to people who have moved for a short time. If so, have you told the church council about those people?

   c. Have other churches told you about members who have moved into your area? If so, have you visited those people?

6. Does your council do all it can to get the church involved in **evangelism**?

—see Church Order, Art. 41

## Church Visitors

Once a year, **church visitors** will visit each church in a classis. The classis will appoint these visitors. They will usually be two experienced ministers. Or they may be a minister and an elder. If the classis needs more visitors, it may decide to appoint another pair.

The visitors' job is to find out if the local churches are being faithful in their ministry. Classis wants to know if the churches are doing what they should. It wants to know if they are preaching and teaching the Word of God correctly. It also wants to know if the churches are following the rules of Church Order. The classis wants to make sure that the members of the churches are growing in their faith and that God's kingdom is growing.

If a local church is not faithfully doing all it should, the church visitors will talk to them as older brothers, giving them advice and help where they can.

If a local church has a serious problem, it can ask the church visitors to come and help with the problem. The local church does not have to wait for the yearly visit.

The church visitors are to give the classis a report of their work.

—see Church Order, Art. 42

## Licensing to Exhort

The classis may allow certain people to **exhort** (explain the Word of God) in worship services. The classis may license these persons if there is an urgent need for their help. This is usually for a short period of time.

These persons do not have to be **ordained**. But they must have the gifts to preach. They must also know the Bible and live for God. And their message must help the church members grow in their faith.

—see Church Order, Art. 43

## Working Together with Nearby Classes

Sometimes a classis has to handle the same issue that a nearby classis has to deal with. When that happens, each classis may give advice to the other. The classes may also work together on the issue.

Classes that work together to deal with the same issue may set themselves up as a separate assembly. This assembly will work like a classis. It may have meetings. It may also call **delegates** from each classis to these meetings.

The purpose of this assembly needs to be approved by synod. Its authority needs to be approved by synod. Synod also has to approve how many classes this assembly may have authority over. This assembly may speak directly to synod about issues that relate to its purpose. (*Note*: Supplement, Article 44-b, of the Church Order gives guidelines for an assembly like this.)

—see Church Order, Art. 44; Supplement, Art. 44-b

## D. The Synod

### Makeup of the Synod

The synod is the assembly that makes decisions for all the classes. This means it makes decisions for *all the churches*. Each classis sends two ministers and two elders as delegates to synod.

*Denominational Funding*

Each synod needs to set a budget for the CRC for the next year. It also needs to approve the amounts of **ministry shares**. These amounts cover the costs of the budget.

Each synod must also approve the budget of every **CRC agency** for the next year. Along with this, the synod must also approve the ministry shares that the agencies ask for.

After each synod, the **director of finances** will tell the treasurer of each classis what the new ministry shares are for that classis.

—see Church Order, Art. 45; Supplement, Art. 45

## Meetings of Synod

Synod meets once a year. The place and date of the meeting is set at the previous synod. Synod asks a local church to call the delegates together for worship before synod begins. This church is called the "convening church."

The "convening church" may call for a special meeting of synod. But it may do this only in a very unusual situation. It needs to have the meeting approved by the synodical **interim committee**.

When synod meets, it elects new officers (president, vice-president, first clerk, and second clerk). These officers must be elected in line with the Rules for Synodical Procedure. The officers must also do their work in line with those rules. (The Rules for Synodical Procedure are published every year along with the standard Church Order.)

—see Church Order, Art. 46

## The Task of Synod

Part of synod's job is to approve the following:

- the **creeds**
- the Church Order
- forms used in worship
- the *Psalter Hymnal*
- the basic principles and parts of worship
- the Bible versions used in the local churches

Sometimes synod will vote to make a major change in one of these. If it does that, synod has to make sure that all the churches have time to think about the change. They also need time to talk about it. Then synod may decide whether or not to make the change final.

*Rules about "Major Changes"*

1. A "major change" is anything that changes the basic meaning of one of the items approved by synod.

2. "Time to think about" and "talk about" the change usually means at least one year. If a synod decides to make a major change, it has to wait for another synod to make a final decision. That synod has to approve ("ratify") the change to make it final. If that synod does not approve the change, then the change is not made.

3. If a synod decides to make any change in one of the items listed above,

   - it must explain clearly what change or changes are being made, and
   - it must say whether the change or changes are "major changes."

—see Church Order, Art. 47; Supplement, Art. 47

## Synodical Deputies

Synod appoints ministers to serve as **synodical deputies**. There is one from each classis. These ministers are first nominated by their classes. They serve as deputies for a period of time set by synod.

Synodical deputies are needed for many decisions, especially at meetings of classis. When they are needed, at least three of them must be present. The Church Order says when synodical deputies are needed.

The synodical deputies will help a classis deal with special problems if it asks for help. The deputies will do this to keep unity, order, and biblical teaching in the churches.

The synodical deputies need to give a report to the next synod about all of their work in the past year.

—see Church Order, Art. 48

### Fellowship with Other Reformed Churches

As the CRC, we want to communicate with other Reformed churches. We want to do this to promote Christian **fellowship** among these churches. We also want to promote unity in the body of Christ. To do this, synod sets up a committee to talk with and work with Reformed churches.

Synod decides what churches we should have fellowship with. Synod also sets up rules for that relationship.

—see Church Order, Art. 49

### Reformed Ecumenical Synods

Sometimes there are large meetings made up of many different Reformed churches. These are called **ecumenical synods**. If we are in **fellowship** with the churches at these meetings, our synod sends **delegates** to them.

Synod may ask those delegates to bring up issues that are important to the CRC. Synod may do this when it wants to see what other churches are thinking about those issues.

These meetings make lots of decisions. We will accept those decisions only if our synod approves them.

—see Church Order, Art. 50

Words in **boldface** type are explained in a glossary at the beginning of this book.

## Part 3: The Activities of the Church

### A. Worship Services

**When and Why We Worship**

Normally all CRC churches will meet at least twice on Sunday for worship. They meet to hear the Word of God. They meet to receive the **sacraments**. They meet to praise God and to pray to God. They also meet to bring their gifts of thanks to God.

Some churches may want to do something in place of the traditional second (or, evening) worship service. Synod encourages those churches to make sure this is part of a strategy for ministry. They should also make sure that in this strategy they are fully accountable to their classis.

Each year there are special holidays when the churches meet for worship. These are Christmas, Good Friday, Easter, Ascension Day, and Pentecost. The churches also worship on Old Year's Day and New Year's Day. They also meet for worship on a day of prayer and a day of thanksgiving.

Sometimes synod may call the churches to have a special worship service. This may be done when we need to pray about great problems in the church, the nation, or the world. It may also be done in times of great blessing.

—see Church Order, Art. 51; Supplement, Art. 51-a

**The Consistory and Worship**

The consistory (elders) watches over all that takes place in the worship services of the local church.

The consistory makes sure that the local church uses the worship materials approved by synod. This includes Bible versions, forms used in worship, and songs.

The consistory makes sure that worship materials that are reshaped to fit the worship style are in line with the rules of synod. The consistory also sees that choirs and other singers use music that is in line with the rules of synod. It does the same with hymns that are not part of the *Psalter Hymnal*, the official song-book of the CRC. So any other hymnal must be approved by the consistory.

*Exception for Churches in Classis Red Mesa*

The consistory (elders) watches over all that takes place in the worship services of the local church.

The consistory makes sure that the local church uses the worship materials approved by synod or classis. This includes Bible versions, forms used in worship, and hymnals.

The consistory makes sure that the basic principles and parts of worship are followed. This must be done in line with the rules of synod or classis.

The consistory makes sure that all hymns used in worship are faithful to God's Word, the Bible.

—see Church Order, Art. 52; Supplement, Art. 52

**Leading the Worship Services**

The ministers of the Word are to lead the worship services.

A person who has a **license to exhort** (explain the Word of God) may lead a worship service. The consistory (elders) may also ask someone to read a sermon and lead a worship service. But these persons may not do any of the official acts that a minister may do.

The consistory must first approve the sermons that are read in the worship service.

*Exception for Churches in Classis Red Mesa*

The minister of the Word will lead the worship service. An **evangelist** may do this too. If a minister or evangelist is not available, the consistory (elders) may ask someone who has a license to exhort to lead in worship. Or one of the elders may lead the worship service.

—see Church Order, Art. 53; Supplement, Art. 53

## Preaching

In the worship service the minister of the Word explains the Word of God. He also applies it to the lives of the church members.

In one of the worship services on Sunday, the minister will preach a sermon that reflects on a part of the **Heidelberg Catechism**. The sermon will be based on a Bible text—a text related to that part of the catechism.

—see Church Order, Art. 54

## Celebrating the Sacraments

The consistory (elders) watches over the way the **sacraments** are celebrated. The sacraments are celebrated only in **public worship**. The minister may lead in celebrating the sacraments. He may do this using the special forms approved by synod. Or he may use forms that are reshaped to fit the worship style, as long as these forms are in line with the rules of synod.

—see Church Order, Art. 55

## Infant Baptism

Children of believers will be baptized as members of God's covenant. The consistory (elders) is to make sure that parents bring their children for **baptism**. The consistory must also see that baptism is held as soon as possible.

—see Church Order, Art. 56

## Adult Baptism

Some adults who come into the church were not baptized as children. They must be baptized when they **profess their faith** at a public worship service. The form for the baptism of adults is to be used for a profession like this.

—see Church Order, Art. 57

## Accepting a Person's Baptism

If a person has been baptized in another Christian church, the local church will decide if it can accept that baptism. The baptism must have been done in the name of God the Father, God the Son, and God the Holy Spirit. It must also have been done by a person authorized by that **denomination**.

—see Church Order, Art. 58

### Becoming Confessing Members and Confessing Adult Members of the Church

Baptized members may become **confessing members** if they profess their faith at a public worship service. This means they may celebrate the **Lord's Supper** with the other confessing members of the church. The **profession of faith** uses a written form based on the Reformed **creeds**.

Before you profess your faith, you first have to meet with the consistory (elders). They ask you why you want to profess your faith. They ask questions about your beliefs and your Christian walk.

If the consistory approves, your name is given to the rest of the church for approval. This is done at least one Sunday before you profess your faith at a worship service.

When a confessing member becomes 18 years old, he or she may make a commitment to the creeds of the CRC and to the responsibilities of adult membership. Then he or she will be given the full rights and privileges of a **confessing adult member**.

Persons who are confessing members of a church in the CRC may become confessing members of another church in the CRC. They may do this when their church sends their membership papers to their new church. These papers need to include a statement about their beliefs and Christian walk.

Persons who are confessing members of another Reformed or **Presbyterian** church may become confessing members of a local CRC church. They may do this after the consistory approves their membership papers from their old church. These papers need to include a statement about their beliefs and Christian walk.

Persons who are confessing members of other denominations may also become confessing members of a CRC church. But the consistory has to examine them to approve them. The consistory will examine them in terms of their beliefs and Christian walk.

In either case, the consistory will decide one of three things:

- to let the persons join as they are,
- to have them reaffirm their faith, or
- to have them profess their faith.

Then their names will be given to the rest of the church for approval.

—see Church Order, Art. 59

### When and How to Celebrate the Lord's Supper

The local church will celebrate the **Lord's Supper** at least once every three months.

The consistory (elders) will decide just how to celebrate the Lord's Supper. They must be sure it follows the Bible's teachings on the Lord's Supper.

—see Church Order, Art. 60

The Church Order is printed at the back of this book (gray pages). **43**

### Prayer in Public Worship

The prayers in **public worship** will include praise, confession, thanks, and requests to God. They will also include requests for all Christians and all people. Synod has approved written prayers that may be used during worship.

—see Church Order, Art. 61

### Offerings

In worship services the **deacons** will collect regular offerings to help people in need. The deacons will also collect other offerings for the ministries of the local church. They will also collect offerings for ministries of the classis and **denomination**.

—see Church Order, Art. 62

## B. Helping Faith Grow

### Helping Children and Youth Grow in Faith

The local church is to help its youth grow in faith and trust in Jesus Christ. They need a personal faith in Christ as their Savior and Lord. The church may also help the youth of the community grow in this way.

To help the faith of these youth to grow, the church will

- receive them in love,
- pray for them,
- teach them in the faith, and
- build them up as members of the body of believers.

In this way the church will help the youth get ready to profess their faith. This will also give them everything they need to live as Christians in the church and in the world.

The local church is to teach these youth about the Bible. It must do this in line with the **creeds** and **confessions**, especially the **Heidelberg Catechism**. The consistory (elders) will supervise this teaching.

—see Church Order, Art. 63

### Helping Adults Grow in Faith

The local church must help its adult members grow in the faith. They need to keep learning about the Lord Jesus as their Savior. They need to grow to mature faith in Christ. They also need to be built up as members of the body of believers.

The consistory (elders) will see that the church offers training that meets the needs of the adult members.

—see Church Order, Art. 64

## C. Pastoral Care

### Giving Pastoral Care

The minister, elders, and deacons of the local church are to give pastoral care to the church members. They should also give pastoral care to others touched by the local church. To do this, the members of council need to visit with people and encourage them in their faith. At least once a year they should make a special visit to all members. The council needs to help those who have drifted away from the truth in their belief or their way of life. It also needs to bring comfort or help to people in need.

—see Church Order, Art. 65

### Transfer of Membership

Sometimes members of a local church move to another CRC church. These persons have the right to a letter of transfer from their council. The council sends membership papers and a statement about each person's beliefs and Christian walk. The letter must state whether the persons are **baptized members**, **confessing members**, or **confessing adult members**. These items are usually mailed to the council of the persons' new church.

All membership papers must be signed by the president and clerk of the council.

—see Church Order, Art. 66; Supplement, Art. 66-a

### Lapse of Membership

When members move to a place where there is no CRC church, they may keep their membership at their home church. Or they may decide to have their membership papers sent to the CRC church that is closest to their new home.

*Rules about Lapsed Membership*

Sometimes people move far away from their home church—so far that they cannot have **fellowship** with that church anymore. But they may still keep their membership at that church, if they ask the consistory (elders) to let them. Their request needs to be approved by the consistory.

These people may also ask to have their membership moved to another CRC church near the place where they have moved.

If these people do not ask for either of these things, the consistory must try hard to get them to do one or the other. But if nothing has been decided after two years, the consistory may decide to **lapse** their membership. This means they are no longer thought of as members of that church. The consistory must try hard to reach these people to tell them what has happened.

This rule does not apply to a member who is away but plans to come back (like someone who has gone to college).

*Rules on Lapsing Members Who Do Not Attend or Support the Church*

Sometimes a member does not worship with the local church anymore and does not support the church anymore. The membership of this person may be lapsed. The consistory may decide to do this if

- the person still claims to be a Christian,
- the person claims to be worshiping at another church, and
- the consistory is not aware of any sin that the person should be **disciplined** for.

The consistory will tell the other members of the church about the lapsed membership. The consistory will also let the person know of its decision.

—see Church Order, Art. 67; Supplement, Art. 67

### Records of Membership

The local church must keep records on
- births,
- deaths,
- **baptisms,**
- **professions of faith,**
- members who come from other churches,
- members who leave the church,
- members who are **lapsed,**
- members who are **excommunicated**, and
- members who come back into the church again.

—see Church Order, Art. 68

### Marriage Ceremonies

The consistory (elders) must teach and advise the church members to marry only other Christians.

A Christian wedding may take place in a worship service or in a private gathering of relatives and friends. The wedding will include proper instructions to the couple. The couple will make promises before God. Prayers will be offered as well, in line with the approved forms for marriage.

A minister may not perform a marriage that would be against the Word of God.

—see Church Order, Art. 69

### Funerals

A funeral is not an official ceremony of the church. A funeral is arranged by the family.

—see Church Order, Art. 70

### Christian Schools

The council is to urge the church members to set up and support good Christian schools. The council is also to encourage parents to send their children to these schools. We believe God calls for this in the covenant of grace.

—see Church Order, Art. 71

## Groups for Youth and Adults

The council is to promote groups that study the Bible. These should be groups for youth and adults. The council should be sure to give advice and support to youth organizations (such as Dynamic Youth Ministries). The council will supervise all these groups in the local church.

—see Church Order, Art. 72

## D. Missions

### The Church's Call to Missions

The Great Commission calls us to bring the good news of Jesus to all who have not heard it (Matthew 28:18-20). The goal is to lead people to accept Christ as their Savior and to become members of his body, the church.

To do this, each council is to encourage the members of the local church to witness for Christ. The members can witness by their words and actions wherever they are. They can support the work of missions in North America and far away. Church members need to show interest in missions. They also need to pray and give for the work of missions everywhere.

—see Church Order, Art. 73

### The Mission of the Congregation

The local church needs to bring the good news of Jesus to people in its community. The council will supervise this work. Sometimes a local church will do this with other local churches in its community.

Each local church will have a ministry of mercy. The **deacons** are to make sure that people in need are cared for by Christian agencies, if possible. The deacons may also need to work with deacons of other CRC churches to help people. They may also work with community agencies to get help for people in need.

—see Church Order, Art. 74

### The Mission of Classis

The classes are to help the local churches in spreading the good news of Jesus, when needed. The classes may also have their own programs for doing this work, to reach beyond the resources of the local churches. For this purpose, each classis will have its own home-missions committee.

The classes are to help the local churches in their ministry of mercy, when needed. The classes may also have their own ministry of mercy, to reach beyond the resources of the local churches. For this purpose, each classis will have its own **diaconal** (deacons) **committee**.

—see Church Order, Art. 75

### CRC Ministries in North America

Synod will encourage and help the churches and classes in their work of **evangelism** (bringing the good news of Jesus). Synod will also do evangelism work that goes beyond the resources of the local churches and classes. For this purpose, synod has a **denominational** home-missions committee. The work of this committee is governed by the rules of synod.

Synod will encourage and help the churches and classes in their ministry of mercy. Synod will also carry on a ministry of mercy that goes beyond the resources of the local churches and classes. For this purpose, synod has a denominational diaconal committee. The work of this committee is governed by the rules of synod.

These "rules of synod" are found in the "Mission Order" statement of Christian Reformed Home Missions.

—see Church Order, Art. 76; Supplement, Art. 76

### CRC Ministries around the World

Synod decides where the CRC will carry out its work of missions around the world. Synod also decides how this is to be done. Synod provides the funds for doing this work. Synod also encourages the local churches to call and support missionaries. To do all this work, synod has a denominational world-missions committee. The work of this committee is governed by the rules of synod. These "rules of synod" are found in the "Mission Order" statement of Christian Reformed World Missions.

The denominational diaconal committee will carry out the CRC's ministry of mercy around the world. This committee is called the Christian Reformed World Relief Committee.

—see Church Order, Art. 77; Supplement, Art. 77

## Part 4: The Admonition and Discipline of the Church

### A. General Information

**The Purpose of Admonition and Discipline**

The church needs to use **admonition** (advice, correction) and **discipline**. It does this to restore people to live for Christ and to have full **fellowship** in the church. This maintains the holiness of the church. And in doing that, the church maintains the honor of God.

—see Church Order, Art. 78

**Responsibility of Members to One Another**

The members of the local church are responsible to each other in their beliefs and in their Christian walk. They should encourage each other and correct each other in love.

The consistory (elders) must teach and remind the church members that they need to help each other live out their Christian faith. The consistory will also promote a loving fellowship. This will lead people to repent for doing wrong and to come back to full fellowship with Christ and the church.

—see Church Order, Art. 79

**Authority of the Consistory**

The consistory (elders) has the authority of Christ to discipline members who have sinned in their teaching or their way of life. The consistory also has this authority in the area of sins that Jesus talks about in Matthew 18:15-17.

—see Church Order, Art. 80

### B. Admonition and Discipline of Members

**No Longer Having Membership and Becoming Restored Again**

Members who have sinned in their way of life or in their teaching will be discipled (taught) by the consistory (elders). If these members continue in their sin, they may no longer be members in the church of Christ.

Baptized persons who no longer have membership may come back into the church of Christ. To do this, they must repent of their sin and profess their faith at a **public worship** service.

Persons who were **confessing members** but who no longer have membership may come back into the church of Christ. To do this, they must repent of their sin.

The consistory will tell the rest of the church when someone no longer has membership. It will also say when someone is coming back into the church. In either case, the consistory will encourage the church to pray for the person and to talk with the person.

—see Church Order, Art. 81

If someone charges a person with doing something wrong, the consistory (elders) needs to look into the charges carefully. The person must also be allowed to defend himself or herself. Only then may the consistory decide to use discipline.

If the person rejects the consistory's advice and correction, he or she will lose the privileges of being a confessing member or a confessing adult member.

A consistory may not take away these privileges unless it gets approval from the classis.

When the classis looks at the case, it must

- decide if the right procedure was followed,
- make sure the consistory has given the person enough pastoral care, and
- decide if the consistory has good reasons for using discipline.

If the classis approves the discipline, the consistory may still decide not to use it. It is always possible that a person may repent and come back into full fellowship.

There are forms and announcements for discipline. The consistory may use these if it feels they will help the person come to repentance.

(*Note:* See the *Acts of Synod 1991*, pp. 720-723. There you will find changes in the forms and announcements for discipline. There's also a form to use when a person comes back into the church. It's called the form for readmission.)

—see Church Order Supplement, Art. 78-81

## C. Admonition and Discipline of Persons in Office

### Special Discipline

All persons who are in **office** are subject to the general discipline of members (see section B above). They are also subject to special discipline. This includes being **suspended**, which means they may no longer do the duties of their office, usually for a set period of time. This discipline can also include being **deposed** (being removed from office).

—see Church Order, Art. 82

### Reasons for Special Discipline

Persons who are in office will receive special discipline if

- they violate the Form of Subscription (see Church Order, Art. 5),
- they do not carry out their duties (see Church Order, Art. 12-18, 23-25),
- they abuse their authority, or
- they do not live by the Bible's teachings and by God's will.

—see Church Order, Art. 83

### Returning to Office

Persons who have been *suspended* or *deposed* from office (see "Special Discipline" above) may return to office. But they may do this only if

- they show they have repented, and
- the church agrees that they can do their tasks as they should without becoming a stumbling block to others.

—see Church Order, Art. 84

*Guidelines for Confidentiality*

When a person is being suspended or deposed, everything must be done with **confidentiality**. This means no one may go around talking about the situation.

Every church must tell its members exactly what is expected of them. This includes what will happen if they are someday corrected and disciplined. It also includes what they should do if another person is corrected and disciplined (see paragraph 4 of section B above).

People who are in office are bound to strict confidentiality. Needy persons come to them for counsel and help. And the elders deal with discipline. A person in office may not talk with other church members about any matters that are brought to them in confidence.

The consistory (elders) will keep careful and confidential records of any discipline it gives. It will also keep track of announcements that are made to the rest of the local church.

The consistory will choose its words carefully when it makes an announcement about a discipline case. The sin of the person is not mentioned, only that he or she is not repentant.

The elders should follow the rules set up for discipline and for public announcements.

—see Church Order Supplement, Art. 78-84

*Guidelines for Admonition and Discipline of Persons in Office*

Persons who are in office must first be *suspended* before they receive general discipline (see section B above).

Sometimes it will be necessary to *depose* persons from office without *suspending* them first. The council or classis that handles the case will decide if that is necessary.

Special discipline of elders, deacons, and evangelists:

- The council may suspend or depose an elder, deacon, or evangelist. The council may do this if another council agrees to it. The other council must be from the nearest church in the same classis.
- If the other council does not agree, then the one council must change its decision or take the issue to classis.

Special discipline of ministers:

- The council may suspend a minister of the Word. The council may do this if another council agrees to it. The other council must be from the nearest church in the same classis.
- If the other council does not agree, then the one council must change its decision or take the issue to classis.

- A minister may not be deposed without the approval of classis and the synodical deputies.

Ministers who work with two councils:

- In some cases, a minister works in one church, and his credentials are with his calling church. In a case like that, the councils of both churches may correct and discipline him. One council may start the process, but not without talking to the other council first.
- If the two councils do not agree, then the issue must go to the classis of the calling church.

The assembly that starts a suspension will be the one to undo it, if that can be done.

The council of the church that has deposed a minister will be the one to say he is available for a call again, if that is possible. The council may do this if the classis and synodical deputies agree. This classis must be the one that approved the deposing of the minister. When the minister accepts a call, he has to be **ordained** again.

—see Church Order Supplement, Art. 82-84

## Conclusion

### Equality of Churches and Officebearers

No church may act as if it is more important than another church. No person in office may act as if he or she is more important than another. All are equal under the authority of Christ.

—see Church Order, Art. 85

### Changing the Church Order

The Church Order is adopted by general agreement at synod. It must be followed faithfully. Only synod may change it.

—see Church Order, Art. 86

# CHURCH ORDER OF THE CHRISTIAN REFORMED CHURCH IN NORTH AMERICA

*Note:* Portions of the Church Order that are printed in *italics* are to be considered for ratification at a later synod.

## INTRODUCTION

*Article 1*

a. The Christian Reformed Church, confessing its complete subjection to the Word of God and the Reformed creeds as a true interpretation of this Word, acknowledging Christ as the only head of his church, and desiring to honor the apostolic injunction that in the churches all things are to be done decently and in order (1 Cor. 14:40), regulates its ecclesiastical organization and activities in the following articles.

b. The main subjects treated in this Church Order are: The Offices of the Church, The Assemblies of the Church, The Task and Activities of the Church, and The Admonition and Discipline of the Church.

## I. THE OFFICES OF THE CHURCH

### A. General Provisions

*Article 2*

The church recognizes the offices of minister of the Word, elder, deacon, and evangelist. These offices differ from each other only in mandate and task, not in dignity and honor.

*Article 3*

a. Confessing male members of the church who meet the biblical requirements are eligible for the offices of minister, elder, and evangelist.

—Cf. Supplement, Article 3-a

b. All confessing members of the church who meet the biblical requirements are eligible for the office of deacon.

c. Only those who have been officially called and ordained or installed shall hold and exercise office in the church.

*Article 4*

a. In calling and electing to an office, the council shall ordinarily present to the congregation a nomination of at least twice the number to be elected. When the council submits a nomination which totals less than twice the number to be elected, it shall give reasons for doing so.

—Cf. Supplement, Article 4-a

b. Prior to making nominations the council may give the congregation an opportunity to direct attention to suitable persons.

c. The election by the congregation shall take place under the supervision of the council after prayer and in accordance with the regulations established by the council. The right to vote shall be limited to confessing members in good standing.

d. After having called the elected persons to their respective offices and having announced their names, the council shall proceed to ordain or install them if no valid impediment has arisen. The ordination or installation shall take place in the public worship services with the use of the prescribed ecclesiastical forms.

*Article 5*

All officebearers, on occasions stipulated by conciliar, classical, and synodical regulations, shall signify their agreement with the doctrine of the church by signing the Form of Subscription.

—Cf. Supplement, Article 5

## B. The Ministers of the Word

*Article 6*

a. The completion of a satisfactory theological training shall be required for admission to the ministry of the Word.

b. Graduates of the theological seminary of the Christian Reformed Church who have been declared candidates for the ministry of the Word by the churches shall be eligible for call.

c. Those who have been trained elsewhere shall not be eligible for call unless they have met the requirements stipulated in the synodical regulations and have been declared by the churches to be candidates for the ministry of the Word.

—Cf. Supplement, Article 6

*Article 7*

a. Those who have not received the prescribed theological training but who give evidence that they are singularly gifted as to godliness, humility, spiritual discretion, wisdom, and the native ability to preach the Word, may, by way of exception, be admitted to the ministry of the Word, especially when the need is urgent.

b. The classis, in the presence of the synodical deputies, shall examine these men concerning the required exceptional gifts. With the concurring advice of the synodical deputies, classis shall proceed as circumstances may warrant and in accordance with synodical regulations.

—Cf. Supplement, Article 7

*Article 8*

a. Ministers of the Christian Reformed Church are eligible for call, with due observance of the relevant rules.

b. Ministers of other denominations desiring to become ministers in the Christian Reformed Church shall be declared eligible for a call by a classis only after a thorough examination of their theological training, ministerial record, knowledge of and soundness in the Reformed faith, and their exemplariness of life. The presence and concurring advice of the synodical deputies are required.

c. Ministers of other denominations who have not been declared eligible for a call shall not be called unless all synodical requirements have been met.

—Cf. Supplement, Article 8

*Article 9*

In nominating and calling a minister, the council shall seek the approval of the counselor who acts in behalf of classis to see that the ecclesiastical regulations have been observed. The council and counselor shall sign the letter of call and the counselor shall render an account of his labors to classis.

*Article 10*

a. The ordination of a candidate for the ministry of the Word requires the approval of the classis of the calling church and of the synodical deputies. The classis, in the presence of the deputies, shall examine him concerning his doctrine and life in accordance with synodical regulations. The ordination shall be accompanied by the laying on of hands by the officiating minister.

b. The installation of a minister shall require the approval of the classis of the calling church or its interim committee, to which the minister shall have previously presented good ecclesiastical testimonials of doctrine and life which have been given him by his former council and classis.

—Cf. Supplement, Article 10

*Article 11*

The calling of a minister of the Word is to proclaim, explain, and apply Holy Scripture in order to gather in and build up the members of the church of Jesus Christ.

*Article 12*

a. A minister of the Word serving as pastor of a congregation shall preach the Word, administer the sacraments, conduct public worship services, catechize the youth, and train members for Christian service. He, with the elders, shall supervise the congregation and his fellow officebearers, exercise admonition and discipline, and see to it that everything is done decently and in order. He, with the elders, shall exercise pastoral care over the congregation, and engage in and promote the work of evangelism.

b. A minister of the Word who enters into the work of missions or is appointed directly by synod shall be called in the regular manner by a local church, which acts in cooperation with the appropriate committees of classis or synod.

c. A minister of the Word may also serve the church in other work which relates directly to his calling, but only after the calling church has demonstrated to the satisfaction of classis, with the concurring advice of the synodical deputies, that said work is consistent with the calling of a minister of the Word.

—Cf. Supplement, Article 12-c

## Article 13

a. A minister of the Word is directly accountable to the calling church, and therefore shall be supervised in doctrine, life, and duties by that church. When his work is with other than the calling church, he shall be supervised in cooperation with other congregations, institutions, or agencies involved.

b. A minister of the Word may be loaned temporarily by his calling church to serve as pastor of a congregation outside of the Christian Reformed Church, but only with the approval of classis, the concurring advice of the synodical deputies, and in accordance with the synodical regulations. Although his duties may be regulated in cooperation with the other congregation, the supervision of his doctrine and life rests with the calling church.

—Cf. Supplement, Article 13-b

## Article 14

a. A minister of the Word shall not leave the congregation with which he is connected for another church without the consent of the council.

b. A minister of the Word who resigns from the ministry in the Christian Reformed Church to enter a ministry outside the denomination shall be released from office by the classis with an appropriate declaration reflecting the resigned minister's status and with the concurring advice of the synodical deputies.

—Cf. Supplement, Article 14-b

c. A minister of the Word, once lawfully called, may not forsake his office. He may, however, be released from office to enter upon a nonministerial vocation for such weighty reasons as shall receive the approval of the classis with the concurring advice of the synodical deputies.

d. A minister of the Word who has entered upon a vocation which classis judges to be nonministerial shall be released from his office within one year of that judgment. The concurring advice of the synodical deputies shall be obtained at the time of the judgment.

e. A former minister of the Word who was released from office may be declared eligible for call upon approval of the classis by which such action was taken, with the concurring advice of the synodical deputies. Upon acceptance of a call, he shall be reordained.

*Article 15*

Each church through its council shall provide for the proper support of its minister(s). By way of exception and with the approval of classis, a church and minister may agree that a minister obtain primary or supplemental income by means of other employment. Ordinarily the foregoing exception shall be limited to churches that cannot obtain assistance adequate to support its minister.

—Cf. Supplement, Article 15

*Article 16*

a. A minister who for valid reasons desires a temporary leave of absence from service to the congregation must have the approval of his council, which shall continue to have supervision over him.

b. A minister who for valid reasons desires termination from service to the congregation must have the approval of his council and classis. The council shall provide for his support in such a way and for such a time as shall receive the approval of classis.

c. A minister of the Word who has been released from active ministerial service to his congregation shall be eligible for a call for a period of two years, after which time the classis, with the concurring advice of the synodical deputies, shall declare him to be released from the ministerial office. For weighty reasons the classis, with the concurring advice of the synodical deputies, may extend his eligibility for call on a yearly basis.

*Article 17*

a. A minister who is neither eligible for retirement nor worthy of discipline may for weighty reasons be released from active ministerial service in his congregation through action initiated by the council. Such release shall be given only with the approval of classis, with the concurring advice of the synodical deputies, and in accordance with synodical regulations.

b. The council shall provide for the support of a released minister in such a way and for such a time as shall receive the approval of classis.

c. A minister of the Word who has been released from active ministerial service in his congregation shall be eligible for call for a period of two years, after which time the classis, with the concurring advice of the synodical deputies, shall declare him to be released from the ministerial office. For weighty reasons the classis, with the concurring advice of the synodical deputies, may extend his eligibility for call on a yearly basis.

—Cf. Supplement, Article 17

*Article 18*

a. A minister who has reached retirement age, or who because of physical or mental disability is incapable of performing the duties of his office, is eligible for retirement. Retirement shall take place with the approval of the council and classis and in accordance with synodical regulations.

b. A retired minister shall retain the honor and title of a minister of the Word and his official connection with the church which he served last, and this church shall be responsible for providing honorably for his support and that of his dependents according to synodical regulations.

c. Should the reasons for his retirement no longer exist, the minister emeritus shall request the council and classis which recommended him for retirement to declare him eligible for call.

—Cf. Supplement, Article 18

*Article 19*

The churches shall maintain a theological seminary at which men are trained for the ministry of the Word. The seminary shall be governed by synod through a board of trustees appointed by synod and responsible to it.

*Article 20*

The task of the ministers of the Word who are appointed as professors of theology is to train the seminary students for the ministry of the Word, expound the Word of God, and vindicate sound doctrine against heresies and errors.

*Article 21*

The churches shall encourage young men to seek to become ministers of the Word and shall grant financial aid to those who are in need of it. Every classis shall maintain a student fund.

*Article 22*

Students who have received licensure according to synodical regulations shall be permitted to exhort in the public worship services.

—Cf. Supplement, Article 22

C. The Evangelists

*Article 23*

a. The evangelist shall be acknowledged as an elder of his calling church with corresponding privileges and responsibilities. His work as elder shall normally be limited to that which pertains to his function as evangelist.

b. Ordinarily, the office of an evangelist working in an emerging congregation will terminate when a group of believers is formed into an organized church. However, upon organization and with the approval of the newly formed council and the classis, the ordained evangelist may continue to serve the newly organized church until an ordained minister is installed or until he has served the newly organized church for a reasonable period of transition.

—Cf. Supplement, Article 23-b

c. An evangelist may also serve an organized congregation along with a minister of the Word.

d. Any service or assignment beyond his specific field of labor requires the authorization of his consistory and the approval of classis.

*Article 24*

a. The task of the evangelist is to witness for Christ and to call for comprehensive discipleship through the preaching of the Word, the administration of the sacraments, evangelism, church education for youth and adults, and pastoral care, in order that the church may be built and unbelievers won for Christ. He shall also equip fellow believers to participate in the work of evangelism.

b. The evangelist shall function under the direct supervision of the council, giving regular reports to it and being present at its meetings whenever possible, particularly when his work is under consideration.

## D. The Elders and Deacons

*Article 25*

a. The elders and deacons shall serve for a limited time as designated by the council. As a rule a specified number of them shall retire from office each year. The retiring officebearers shall be succeeded by others unless the circumstances and the profit of the church make immediate eligibility for reelection advisable. Elders and deacons who are thus reelected shall be reinstalled.

b. The elders, with the minister(s), shall oversee the doctrine and life of the members of the congregation and fellow officebearers, shall exercise admonition and discipline along with pastoral care in the congregation, shall participate in and promote evangelism, and shall defend the faith.

c. The deacons shall represent and administer the mercy of Christ to all people, especially to those who belong to the community of believers, and shall stimulate the members of Christ's church to faithful, obedient stewardship of their resources on behalf of the needy—all with words of biblical encouragement and testimony which assure the unity of word and deed.

## II. THE ASSEMBLIES OF THE CHURCH

### A. General Provisions

*Article 26*

The assemblies of the church are the council, the classis, and the synod.

*Article 27*

a. Each assembly exercises, in keeping with its own character and domain, the ecclesiastical authority entrusted to the church by Christ; the authority of councils being original, that of major assemblies being delegated.

b. The classis has the same authority over the council as the synod has over the classis.

*Article 28*

a. These assemblies shall transact ecclesiastical matters only, and shall deal with them in an ecclesiastical manner.

b. A major assembly shall deal only with those matters which concern its churches in common or which could not be finished in the minor assemblies.

c. Matters referred by minor assemblies to major assemblies shall be presented in harmony with the rules for classical and synodical procedure.

—Cf. Supplement, Article 28

*Article 29*

Decisions of ecclesiastical assemblies shall be reached only upon due consideration. The decisions of the assemblies shall be considered settled and binding, unless it is proved that they conflict with the Word of God or the Church Order.

*Article 30*

a. Assemblies and church members may appeal to the assembly next in order if they believe that injustice has been done or that a decision conflicts with the Word of God or the Church Order. Appellants shall observe all ecclesiastical regulations regarding the manner and time of appeal.

b. Synod may establish rights for other appeals and adopt rules for processing them.

c. If invoked, the Judicial Code shall apply to the processing of appeals and written charges.

—Cf. Supplement, Article 30a-c

*Article 31*

A request for revision of a decision shall be submitted to the assembly which made the decision. Such a request shall be honored only if sufficient and new grounds for reconsideration are presented.

—Cf. Supplement, Article 31

*Article 32*

a. The sessions of all assemblies shall begin and end with prayer.

b. In every assembly there shall be a president whose duty it shall be to state and explain the business to be transacted, and to see to it that the stipulations of the Church Order are followed and that everyone observes due order and decorum in speaking. There shall also be a clerk whose task it shall be to keep an accurate record of the proceedings. In major assemblies the above named offices shall cease when the assembly adjourns.

c. Each assembly shall make proper provision for receiving communications, preparing agenda and acts, keeping files and archives, and conducting the financial transactions of the assembly.

d. Each assembly shall provide for the safeguarding of its property through proper incorporation.

*Article 33*

a. The assemblies may delegate to committees the execution of their decisions or the preparation of reports for future consideration. They shall give every committee a well-defined mandate, and shall require of them regular and complete reports of their work.

b. Each classis shall appoint a classical interim committee, and synod shall appoint a synodical interim committee, to act for them in matters which cannot await action by the assemblies themselves. Such committees shall be given well-defined mandates and shall submit all their actions to the next meeting of the assembly for approval.

*Article 34*

The major assemblies are composed of officebearers who are delegated by their constituent minor assemblies. The minor assemblies shall provide their delegates with proper credentials which authorize them to deliberate and vote on matters brought before the major assemblies. A delegate shall not vote on any matter in which he himself or his church is particularly involved.

## B. The Council

*Article 35*

a. In every church there shall be a council composed of the minister(s), the elders, and the deacons. Those tasks which belong to the common administration of the church, such as the calling of a pastor, the approval of nominations for church office, mutual censure, meeting with church visitors, and other matters of common concern, are the responsibility of the council.

—Cf. Supplement, Article 35-a

b. In every church there shall be a consistory composed of the elders and the minister(s) of the Word. Those tasks which belong distinctively to the office of elder are the responsibility of the consistory.

c. In every church there shall be a diaconate composed of the deacons of the church. Those tasks which belong distinctively to the office of deacon are the responsibility of the diaconate. The diaconate shall give an account of its work to the council.

*Article 36*

a. The council, consistory, and diaconate shall meet at least once a month at a time and place announced to the congregation. A minister shall ordinarily preside at meetings of the council and the consistory, or in the absence of a minister, one of the elders shall preside. The diaconate shall elect a president from among its members.

b. The council, at least four times per year, shall exercise mutual censure, which concerns the performance of the official duties of the officebearers.

*Article 37*

The council, besides seeking the cooperation of the congregation in the election of officebearers, shall also invite its judgment about other major matters, except those which pertain to the supervision and discipline of the congregation. For this purpose the council shall call a meeting at least annually of all members entitled to vote. Such a meeting shall be conducted by the council, and only those matters which it presents shall be considered. Although full consideration shall be given to the judgment expressed by the congregation, the authority for making and carrying out final decisions remains with the council as the governing body of the church.

*Article 38*

a. Groups of believers among whom no council can as yet be constituted shall be under the care of a neighboring council, designated by classis.

b. When a council is being constituted for the first time, the approval of classis is required.

## C. The Classis

*Article 39*

A classis shall consist of a group of neighboring churches. The organizing of a new classis and the redistricting of classes require the approval of synod.

—Cf. Supplement, Article 39

*Article 40*

a. The council of each church shall delegate a minister and an elder to the classis. If a church is without a minister, or the minister is prevented from attending, two elders shall be delegated. Officebearers who are not delegated may also attend classis and may be given an advisory voice.

b. The classis shall meet at least every four months, unless great distances render this impractical, at such time and place as was determined by the previous classical meeting.

c. The ministers shall preside in rotation, or a president may be elected from among the delegates; however, the same person shall not preside twice in succession.

—Cf. Supplement, Article 40-a and c

*Article 41*

In order properly to assist the churches, the president, on behalf of classis, shall among other things present the following questions to the delegates of each church:

1. Are the council, consistory, and diaconate meetings regularly held according to the needs of the congregation?

2. Is church discipline faithfully exercised?

3. Does the diaconate faithfully lead and stimulate the congregation in obedient stewardship of its resources on behalf of the needy?

4. Does the council diligently promote the cause of Christian education from elementary school through institutions of higher learning?

5. a. Have you submitted to the secretary of our Home Missions Board the names and addresses of all baptized and communicant members who have, since the last meeting of classis, moved to a place where no Christian Reformed churches are found?

   b. Have you informed other councils or pastors about members who reside, even temporarily, in the vicinity of their church?

   c. Have you, having been informed yourself of such members in your own area, done all in your power to serve them with the ministry of your church?

6. Does the council diligently engage in and promote the work of evangelism in its community?

*Article 42*

a. The classis shall appoint at least one committee composed of two of the more experienced and competent officebearers, two ministers, or one minister and one elder, to visit all its churches once a year.

b. The church visitors shall ascertain whether the officebearers faithfully perform their duties, adhere to sound doctrine, observe the provisions of the Church Order, and properly promote the edification of the congregation and the extension of God's kingdom. They shall fraternally admonish those who have been negligent, and help all with advice and assistance.

c. The churches are free to call on the church visitors whenever serious problems arise.

d. The church visitors shall render to classis a written report of their work.

*Article 43*

The classis may grant the right to exhort within its bounds to men who are gifted, well-informed, consecrated, and able to edify the churches. When the urgent need for their services has been established, the classis shall examine such men and license them as exhorters for a limited period of time.

*Article 44*

a. A classis may take counsel or joint action with its neighboring classis or classes in matters of mutual concern.

b. Classes engaging in matters of mutual concern may organize themselves into an ecclesiastical assembly that will function on the level of classis, with freedom to determine the delegation from the constituent classes and the frequency of meetings. Such an assembly's authority, jurisdiction, and mandate shall be approved by synod. It shall have direct access to synod in all matters pertaining to its mandate.

—Cf. Supplement, Article 44-b

## D. The Synod

*Article 45*

The synod is the assembly representing the churches of all the classes. Each classis shall delegate two ministers and two elders to the synod.

—Cf. Supplement, Article 45

*Article 46*

a. Synod shall meet annually, at a time and place determined by the previous synod. Each synod shall designate a church to convene the following synod.

b. The convening church, with the approval of the synodical interim committee, may call a special session of synod, but only in very extraordinary circumstances and with the observance of synodical regulations.

c. The officers of synod shall be elected and shall function in accordance with the Rules for Synodical Procedure.

*Article 47*

The task of synod includes the adoption of the creeds, of the Church Order, of the liturgical forms, of the *Psalter Hymnal*, and of the principles and elements of the order of worship, as well as the designation of the Bible versions to be used in the worship services.

No substantial alterations shall be effected by synod in these matters unless the churches have had prior opportunity to consider the advisability of the proposed changes.

—Cf. Supplement, Article 47

*Article 48*

a. Upon the nomination of the classes, synod shall appoint ministers, one from each classis, to serve as synodical deputies for a term designated by synod.

b. When the cooperation of the synodical deputies is required as stipulated in the Church Order, the presence of at least three deputies from the nearest classes shall be prescribed.

c. Besides the duties elsewhere stipulated, the deputies shall, upon request, extend help to the classes in the event of difficulties in order that proper unity, order, and sound doctrine may be maintained.

d. The synodical deputies shall submit a complete report of their actions to the next synod.

*Article 49*

a. Synod shall appoint a committee to correspond with other Reformed churches so that the Christian Reformed Church may exercise Christian fellowship with other denominations and may promote the unity of the church of Jesus Christ.

b. Synod shall decide which denominations are to be received into ecclesiastical fellowship, and shall establish the rules which govern these relationships.

## Article 50

a. Synod shall send delegates to Reformed ecumenical synods in which the Christian Reformed Church cooperates with other denominations which confess and maintain the Reformed faith.

b. Synod may present to such gatherings matters on which it seeks the judgment of the Reformed churches throughout the world.

c. Decisions of Reformed ecumenical synods shall be binding upon the Christian Reformed Church only when they have been ratified by its synod.

## III. THE TASK AND ACTIVITIES OF THE CHURCH

### A. Worship Services

## Article 51

a. The congregation shall assemble for worship, *ordinarily* twice on the Lord's Day, to hear God's Word, to receive the sacraments, to engage in praise and prayer, and to present gifts of gratitude.

—Cf. Supplement, Article 51-a

b. Worship services shall be held in observance of Christmas, Good Friday, Easter, Ascension Day, and Pentecost, and ordinarily on Old and New Year's Day, and annual days of prayer and thanksgiving.

c. Special worship services may be proclaimed in times of great stress or blessing for church, nation, or world.

*Note:* The proposed change in Article 51-a needs to be adopted by Synod 1996.

## Article 52

a. The consistory shall regulate the worship services.

b. The consistory shall see to it that the synodically approved Bible versions, liturgical forms, and songs are used, and that the principles and elements of the order of worship approved by synod are observed.

c. The consistory shall see to it that if liturgical forms are adapted, these adaptations conform to synodical guidelines and that if choirs or others sing in the worship service, they observe the synodical regulations governing the content of the hymns and anthems sung. These regulations shall also apply when supplementary hymns are sung by the congregation.

—Cf. Supplement, Article 52

## Article 53

a. The ministers of the Word shall conduct the worship services.

b. Persons licensed to exhort and anyone appointed by the consistory to read a sermon may conduct worship services. They shall, however, refrain from all official acts of the ministry.

c. Only sermons approved by the consistory shall be read in the worship services.

—Cf. Supplement, Article 53

## Article 54

a. In the worship services the minister of the Word shall officially explain and apply Holy Scripture.

b. At one of the services each Lord's Day, the minister shall ordinarily preach the Word as summarized in the Heidelberg Catechism, following its sequence.

## Article 55

The sacraments shall be administered upon the authority of the consistory in the public worship service, by the minister of the Word, with the use of the prescribed forms or adaptations of them which conform to synodical guidelines.

## Article 56

The covenant of God shall be sealed to children of believers by holy baptism. The consistory shall see to it that baptism is requested and administered as soon as feasible.

## Article 57

Adults who have not been baptized shall receive holy baptism upon public profession of faith. The form for the Baptism of Adults shall be used for such public professions.

## Article 58

The baptism of one who comes from another Christian denomination shall be held valid if it has been administered in the name of the triune God, by someone authorized by that denomination.

## Article 59

a. Members by baptism shall be admitted to the Lord's Supper upon a public profession of their faith in Christ with the use of a prescribed form. Before the profession of faith the consistory shall ensure that there be an appropriate examination concerning their motives, faith, and life. Their membership shall be designated as "confessing member." The names of those who are to be admitted to the Lord's Supper shall be announced to the congregation for approval at least one Sunday before the public profession of faith.

b. Confessing members who have reached the age of eighteen and who have made a commitment to the creeds of the Christian Reformed Church and the responsibilities of adult membership in the church shall be accorded the full rights and privileges of such membership.

c. Confessing members coming from other Christian Reformed congregations shall be admitted to communicant membership upon the presentation of certificates of membership attesting their soundness in doctrine and life.

d. Confessing members coming from churches in ecclesiastical fellowship shall be admitted to communicant membership upon presentation of certificates or statements of membership after the consistory has satisfied itself concerning the doctrine and conduct of the members. Persons coming from other denominations shall be admitted to communicant membership only after the consistory has examined them concerning doctrine and conduct. The consistory shall determine in each case whether to admit them directly or by public reaffirmation or profession of faith. Their names shall be announced to the congregation for approval.

*Article 60*

a. The Lord's Supper shall be administered at least once every three months.

b. The consistory shall provide for such administrations as it shall judge most conducive to edification. However, the ceremonies as prescribed in God's Word shall not be changed.

*Article 61*

a. The public prayers in the worship service shall include adoration, confession, thanksgiving, supplication, and intercession for all Christendom and all men.

b. In the ministry of prayer the approved liturgical prayers may be used.

*Article 62*

Offerings for benevolence shall be received regularly in the worship services. Offerings also shall be received for other ministries of the congregation and the joint ministries of the churches.

### B. Faith Nurture

*Article 63*

a. Each church shall minister to its youth—and to the youth in the community who participate—by nurturing their personal faith and trust in Jesus Christ as Savior and Lord, by preparing them to profess their faith publicly, and by equipping them to assume their Christian responsibilities in the church and in the world. This nurturing ministry shall include receiving them in love, praying for them, instructing them in the faith, and encouraging and sustaining them in the fellowship of believers.

b. Each church shall instruct the youth in the Scriptures and in the creeds and the confessions of the church, especially the Heidelberg Catechism. This instruction shall be supervised by the consistory.

*Article 64*

a. Each church shall minister to its adult members so as to increase their knowledge of the Lord Jesus, to nurture a mature faith in Christ, and to encourage and sustain them in the fellowship of believers.

b. Each church shall provide opportunities for continued instruction of adult members. This instruction shall be supervised by the consistory.

## C. Pastoral Care

*Article 65*

The officebearers of the church shall extend pastoral care to all members of the congregation and to others whenever possible by calling and encouraging them to live by faith, conducting annual home visitation, seeking to restore those who err in doctrine or life, and comforting and giving assistance in adversity.

*Article 66*

a. Confessing members who remove to another Christian Reformed church are entitled to a certificate, issued by the council, concerning their doctrine and life. When such certificates of membership are requested, they shall ordinarily be mailed to the church of their new residence.

—Cf. Supplement, Article 66-a

b. Members by baptism who remove to another Christian Reformed church shall upon proper request be granted a certificate of baptism, to which such notations as are necessary shall be attached. Such certificates shall as a rule be mailed to the church of their new residence.

c. Ecclesiastical certificates shall be signed by the president and clerk of the council.

*Article 67*

Members who move to localities where there is no Christian Reformed church may, upon their request, either retain their membership in the church of their former residence, or have their certificates sent to the nearest Christian Reformed church.

—Cf. Supplement, Article 67

*Article 68*

Each church shall keep a complete record of all births, deaths, baptisms, professions of faith, receptions and dismissals of members, and excommunications and other terminations of membership.

*Article 69*

a. Consistories shall instruct and admonish those under their spiritual care to marry only in the Lord.

b. Christian marriages should be solemnized with appropriate admonitions, promises, and prayers, as provided for in the official form. Marriages may be solemnized either in a worship service, or in private gatherings of relatives and friends.

c. Ministers shall not solemnize marriages which would be in conflict with the Word of God.

*Article 70*

Funerals are not ecclesiastical but family affairs, and should be conducted accordingly.

*Article 71*

The council shall diligently encourage the members of the congregation to establish and maintain good Christian schools, and shall urge parents to have their children instructed in these schools according to the demands of the covenant.

*Article 72*

The council shall promote societies within the congregation for the study of God's Word and shall serve especially the youth organizations with counsel and assistance. All such societies are under the supervision of the council.

D. Missions

*Article 73*

a. In obedience to Christ's Great Commission, the churches must bring the gospel to all men at home and abroad, in order to lead them into fellowship with Christ and his church.

b. In fulfilling this mandate, each council shall stimulate the members of the congregation to be witnesses for Christ in word and deed and to support the work of home and foreign missions by their interest, prayers, and gifts.

*Article 74*

a. Each church shall bring the gospel to unbelievers in its own community. This task shall be sponsored and governed by the council. This task may be executed, when conditions warrant, in cooperation with one or more neighboring churches.

b. Each church shall carry on a ministry of mercy. The deacons shall enable the needy under their care to make use of Christian institutions of mercy. They shall confer and cooperate with diaconates of neighboring churches when this is desirable for the proper performance of their task. They may also seek mutual understandings with agencies in their community which are caring for the needy, so that the gifts may be distributed properly.

*Article 75*

a. The classes shall, whenever necessary, assist the churches in their local evangelistic programs. The classes themselves may perform this work of evangelism when it is beyond the scope and resources of the local churches. To administer these tasks, each classis shall have a classical home missions committee.

b. The classes shall, whenever necessary, assist the churches in their ministry of mercy. The classes themselves may perform this ministry when it is beyond the scope and resources of the local churches. To administer this task, each classis shall have a classical diaconal committee.

*Article 76*

a. Synod shall encourage and assist congregations and classes in their work of evangelism, and shall also carry on such home missions activities as are beyond their scope and resources. To administer these activities synod shall appoint a denominational home missions committee, whose work shall be controlled by synodical regulations.

b. Synod shall encourage and assist congregations and classes in their ministry of mercy, and shall carry on such work as is beyond their scope and resources. Synod shall appoint a diaconal committee to administer the denominational ministry of mercy. The work of this committee shall be governed by synodical regulations.

—Cf. Supplement, Article 76

*Article 77*

a. Synod shall determine the field in which the joint world mission work of the churches is to be carried on, regulate the manner in which this task is to be performed, provide for its cooperative support, and encourage the congregations to call and support missionaries. To administer these activities synod shall appoint a denominational world missions committee, whose work shall be controlled by synodical regulations.

b. The denominational diaconal committee shall extend the ministry of mercy of the congregations and classes worldwide.

—Cf. Supplement, Article 77

## IV. THE ADMONITION AND DISCIPLINE OF THE CHURCH

### A. General Provisions

*Article 78*

The purpose of admonition and discipline is to restore those who err to faithful obedience to God and full fellowship with the congregation, to maintain the holiness of the church, and thus to uphold God's honor.

*Article 79*

a. The members of the church are accountable to one another in their doctrine and life and have the responsibility to encourage and admonish one another in love.

b. The consistory shall instruct and remind the members of the church of their responsibility and foster a spirit of love and openness within the fellowship so that erring members may be led to repentance and reconciliation.

*Article 80*

The consistory shall exercise the authority which Christ has given to his church regarding sins of a public nature or those brought to its attention according to the rule of Matthew 18:15-17.

### B. The Admonition and Discipline of Members

*Article 81*

a. Members who have sinned in life or doctrine shall be faithfully discipled by the consistory and, if they persist in their sin, shall be excluded from membership in the church of Christ.

b. Members by baptism who have been excluded from membership in the church and who later repent of their sin shall be received again into its fellowship upon public profession of faith.

c. Confessing members who have been excluded from membership in the church shall be received again into its fellowship upon repentance of their sin.

d. The consistory shall inform the congregation and encourage its involvement in both the exclusion from and the readmission to membership.

—Cf. Supplement, Articles 78-81

### C. The Admonition and Discipline of Officebearers

*Article 82*

All officebearers, in addition to being subject to general discipline, are subject to special discipline, which consists of suspension and deposition from office.

*Article 83*

Special discipline shall be applied to officebearers if they violate the Form of Subscription, are guilty of neglect or abuse of office, or in any way seriously deviate from sound doctrine and godly conduct.

*Article 84*

Persons who have been suspended or deposed from office may be reinstated if they give sufficient evidence of repentance and if the church judges that they are able to serve effectively.

—Cf. Supplement, Articles 82-84

# CONCLUSION

*Article 85*

No church shall in any way lord it over another church, and no officebearer shall lord it over another officebearer.

*Article 86*

This Church Order, having been adopted by common consent, shall be faithfully observed, and any revision thereof shall be made only by synod.